HILLSIDE CEMETERY

MIDDLETOWN, NEW YORK

BEYOND THE GRAVES

JoEllen Hundeland

AMERICA THROUGH TIME®
ADDING COLOR TO AMERICAN HISTORY

Fonthill Media Inc.
www.fonthillmedia.com
office@fonthillmedia.com

First published 2023

ISBN 978-1-63499-491-0

Typeset in Sabon 10pt on 12pt
Printed and bound in England

CONTENTS

When the dead are alone, they chat very pleasantly amongst themselves and tell each other things; they tell each other their stories. It must be very interesting to live inside a cemetery and hear how the dead tell each other things, their sorrows, their joys, everything.

Eliseo Diego

INTRODUCTION

To understand the significance of Hillside and some of its burials, some knowledge of Middletown, New York, is important. Middletown, about ninety minutes north of New York City in the Hudson Valley, was settled around 1756. By 1843, the Erie Railroad came to town and Middletown went from sleepy hamlet to bustling village. With the plank roads and railroads expanding and boosting prosperity, Middletown became incorporated as a city in 1888. Many new citizens arrived in these industrious years and built their livelihoods here, and although it is impossible to name everyone who left a historical footprint, many of these remarkable individuals are now spending eternity in Hillside Cemetery.

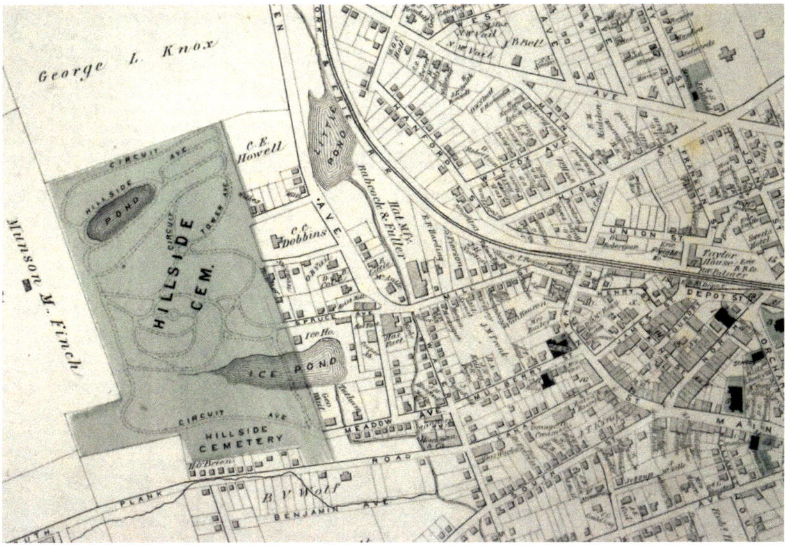

This undated segment of an old Middletown map shows Hillside on the edge of the busy town.

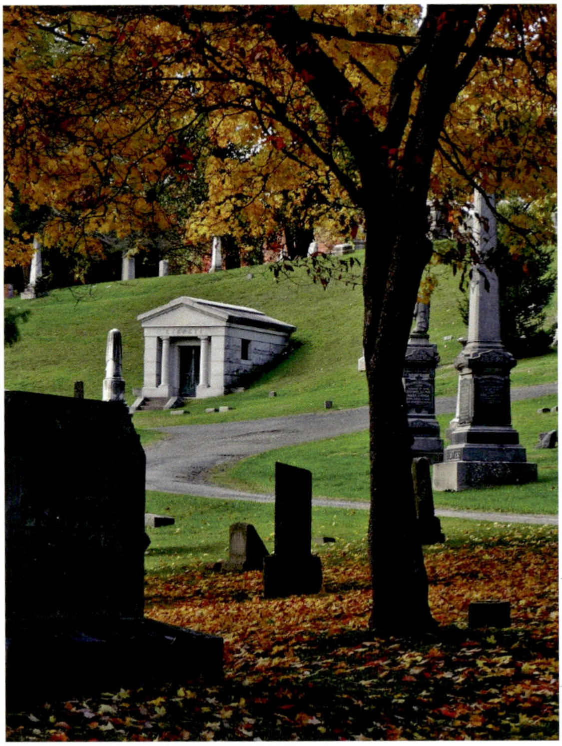

Left: There is nothing more beautiful than Hillside in the autumn months.

Below: At the entrance of the cemetery, a historical marker indicates some of the notable burials in Hillside.

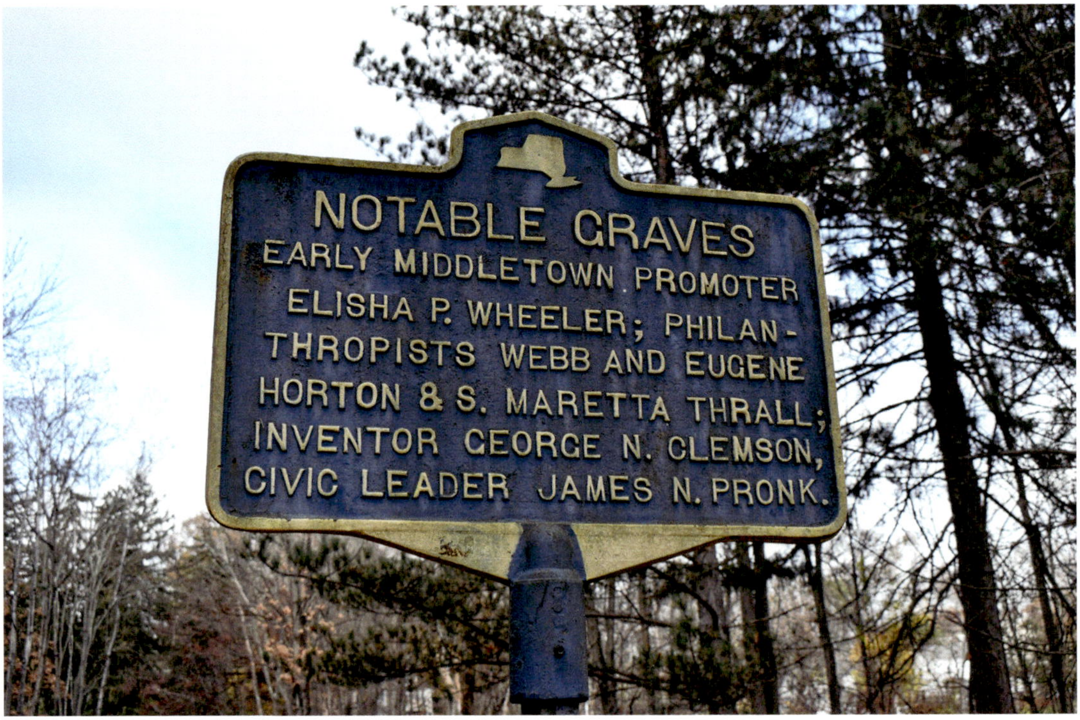

1

Hillside's History

Hillside Cemetery was consecrated in August 1861 due to the efforts of James N. Pronk (1822–1895). A Middletown lawyer, teacher, community leader, and activist, Pronk was involved in many local enterprises; there wasn't an institution or organization he wasn't affiliated with. Pronk was village president for many years. In addition to being instrumental in establishing Hillside, he was also the president of the cemetery association up until his death, proudly supervising every burial that occurred. On August 17, 1895, he fell ill while standing graveside and never returned. According to his obituary: "Beautiful Hillside Cemetery is Mr. Pronk's greatest gift to Middletown." The blue and yellow historical marker near the entrance of Hillside lists Pronk as one of the cemetery's notable graves, and it best describes him as a "civic leader."

As society was tiring of traditional churchyards, Calvert Vaux designed Hillside as a Victorian rural cemetery, which initially included two ponds and miles of carriage trails winding through the trees. Vaux was a noted architect, best known for designing Central Park in New York City. Originally part of the George Houston farm, the new cemetery was 50 rolling acres. Today, Houston's picturesque tract of land is dotted with colossal obelisks, grand mausoleums, stargazing angels, and diverse tombstones.

The first burial in Hillside was Theophilis Vail on September 19, 1861. There is a stone to commemorate this; however, former Hillside board member and cemetery tour guide Ann Vail has said that Moses Vail died on September 6, 1861, almost two weeks before Theophilis.

There are graves in Hillside that are older than the cemetery itself. To make way for urban development, graves from Middletown's first cemetery (located behind the First Congregational Church) were moved to Hillside in 1871. Ninety-eight graves of the town's earliest settlers were moved from the churchyard and reinterred in one grave. Two rows of tombstones bearing the family names of Corwin, McQuoid, Mills, Vail, Horton, Wells, and Moore, including one of Middletown's first settlers, David Moore (1713–1789), still stand today off Hyacinth Path. Also buried here is Capt. Isaiah Vail (1731–1810), who fought in the Revolutionary War.

In 1882, bodies were relocated from Little Cemetery and the adjacent South Middletown Cemetery to Hillside. Not only were these graveyards neglected, but there were intentions for the site to be the future home of Academy Avenue Park. This second move included members of the Beakes, Everett, and Genung families. The Reverend Daniel Thompson Wood (1800–1859) and his wife, Catherine, were moved from Academy Avenue; he was pastor of Middletown's First Presbyterian Church for twenty-nine years until his death. Stacy Beakes, Jr. (1778–1849) founded the first post office inside his general store in 1816. Beakes was also town clerk, town supervisor, first village president, sheriff, and he operated the first distillery. The Beakes name is prominent throughout Middletown history and Hillside. Unlike the burials relocated from the Congregational church, the Academy Avenue graves received their own individual plots in Hillside.

Today, at the entrance of the cemetery, sits an ornate former chapel that is currently used as a residence. Towards the back of the cemetery, there is a walkway of flat tombstones that were discovered during clean-up efforts.

At one time, according to an old Hillside map, there were two ponds on the property. One of the former ponds is still there, although it is hedged by cattails. The other, referred to as Lake Embryo, has long since dried up. There were plans for an observation tower on one of the cemetery's high points; sadly, it was never built. A majestic pine tree stands in its place.

In 1994, Hillside was placed on the National Register of Historic Places, and rightfully so. Not only is Hillside filled with stunning statuary and graceful monuments, but it is also a testament to the community's place in history.

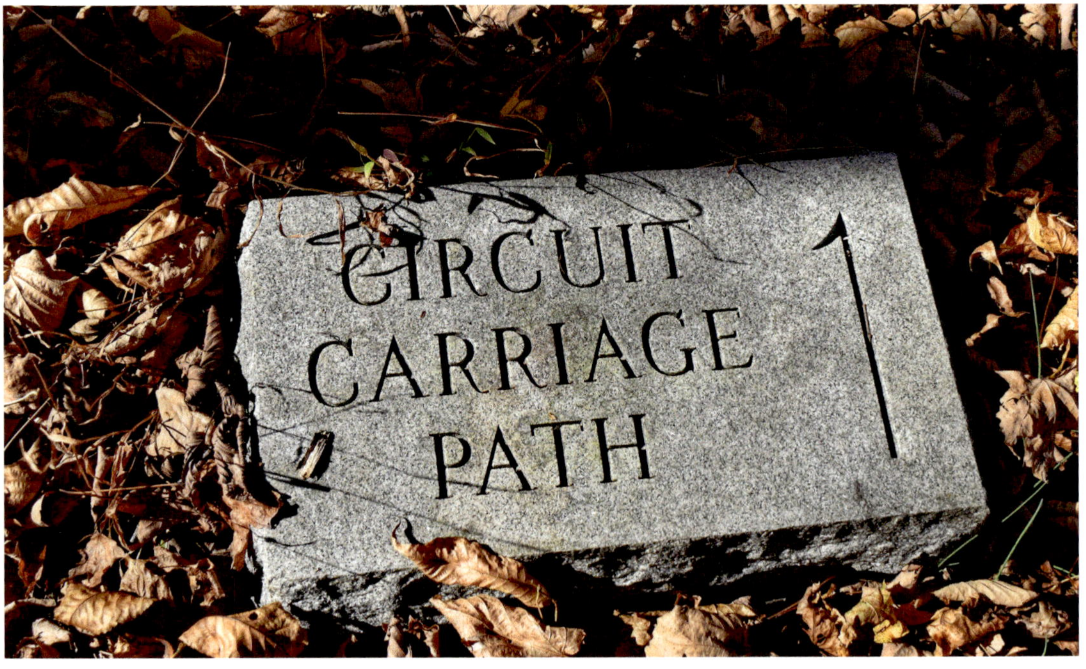

Towards the back edge of the cemetery, a slab marker identifies the original route of the carriage trail.

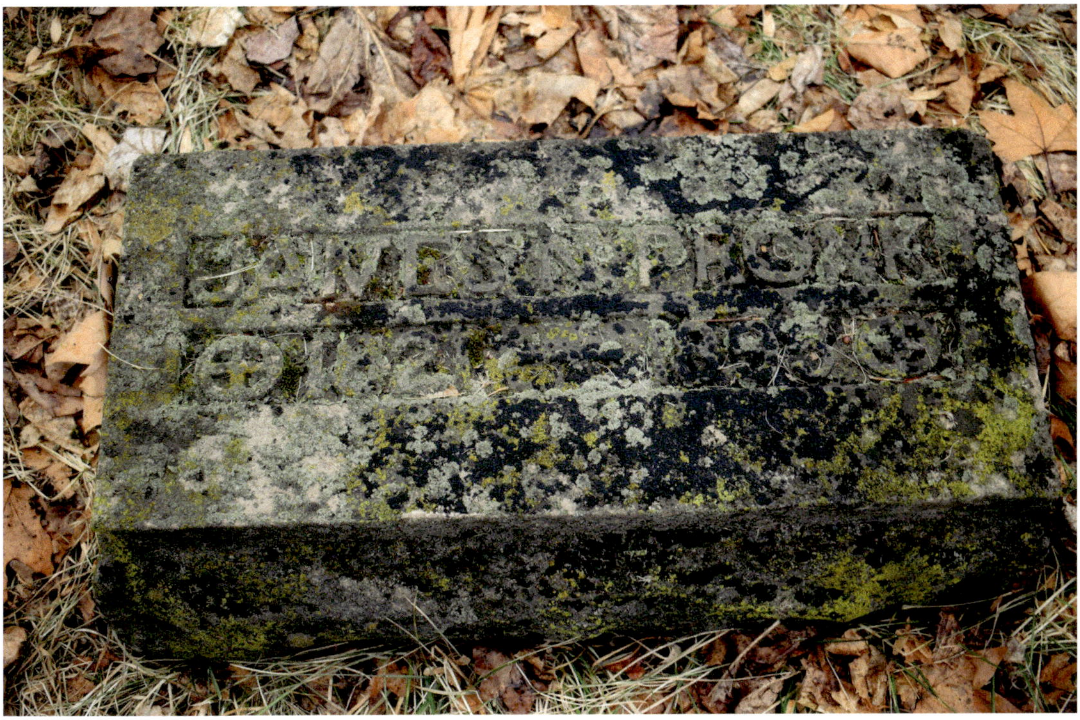

The family plot and grave of James N. Pronk, who is credited with Hillside's founding. His grave is marked with a modest stone in the middle of the cemetery he loved so.

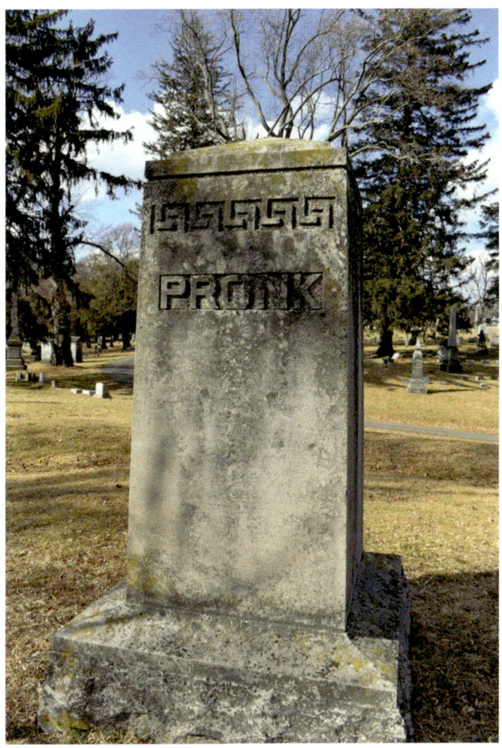

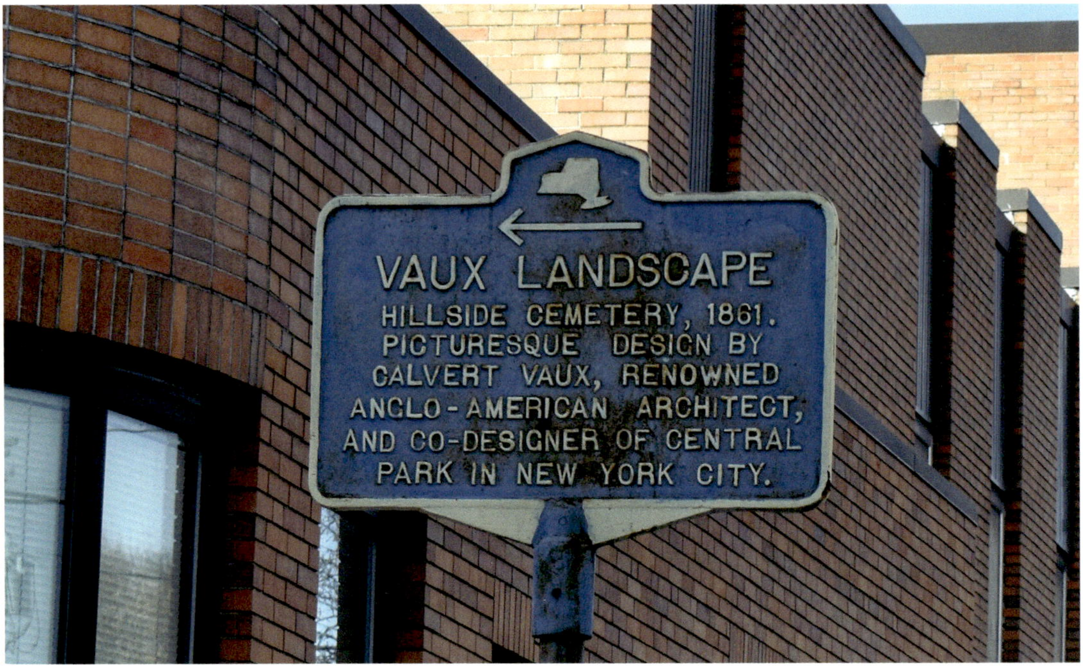

A historical marker paying homage to Calvert Vaux sits at the street corner near Hillside Cemetery.

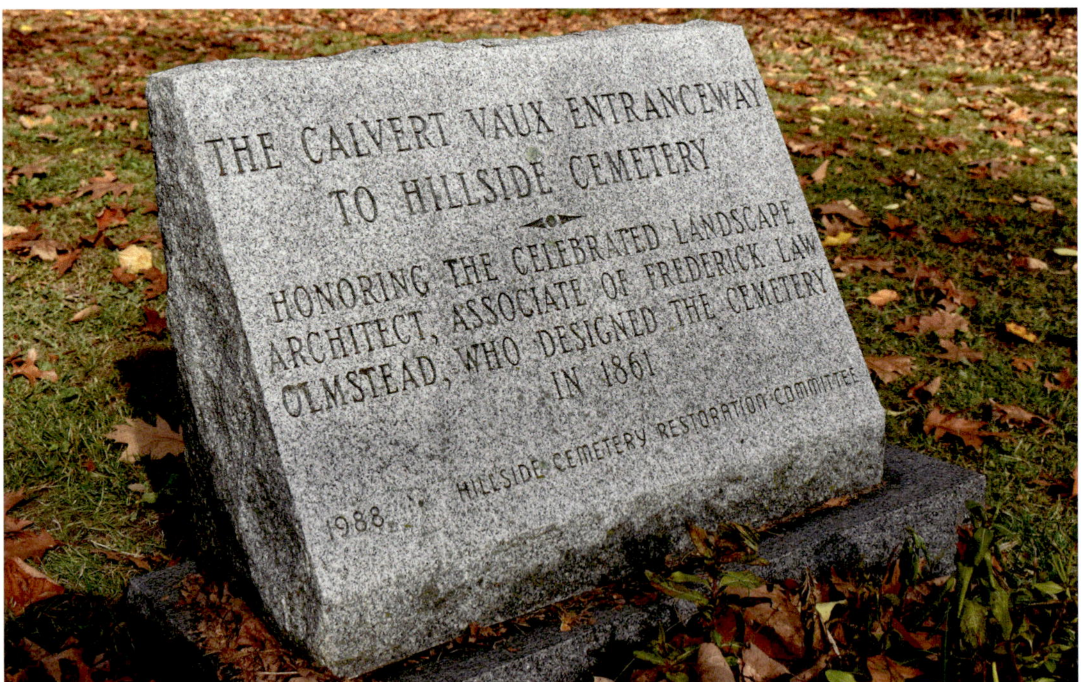

The cemetery also has a marker honoring Vaux along the main entrance.

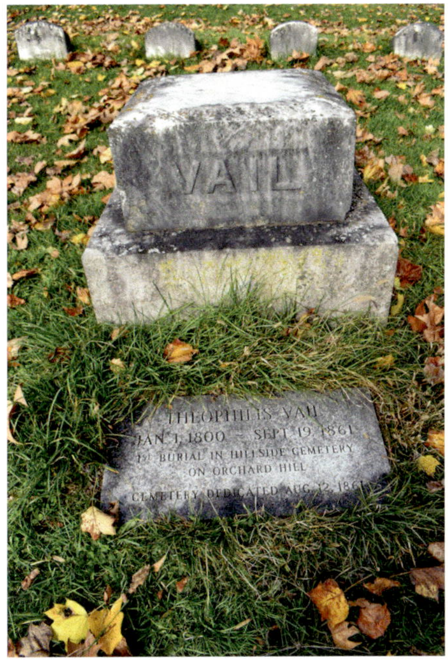

Right: On the slope of Orchard Hill sits the grave of Theophilis Vail, the first known burial in Hillside.

Below: A marker placed off Hyacinth Path reveals the location of the Congregational Church reinterments.

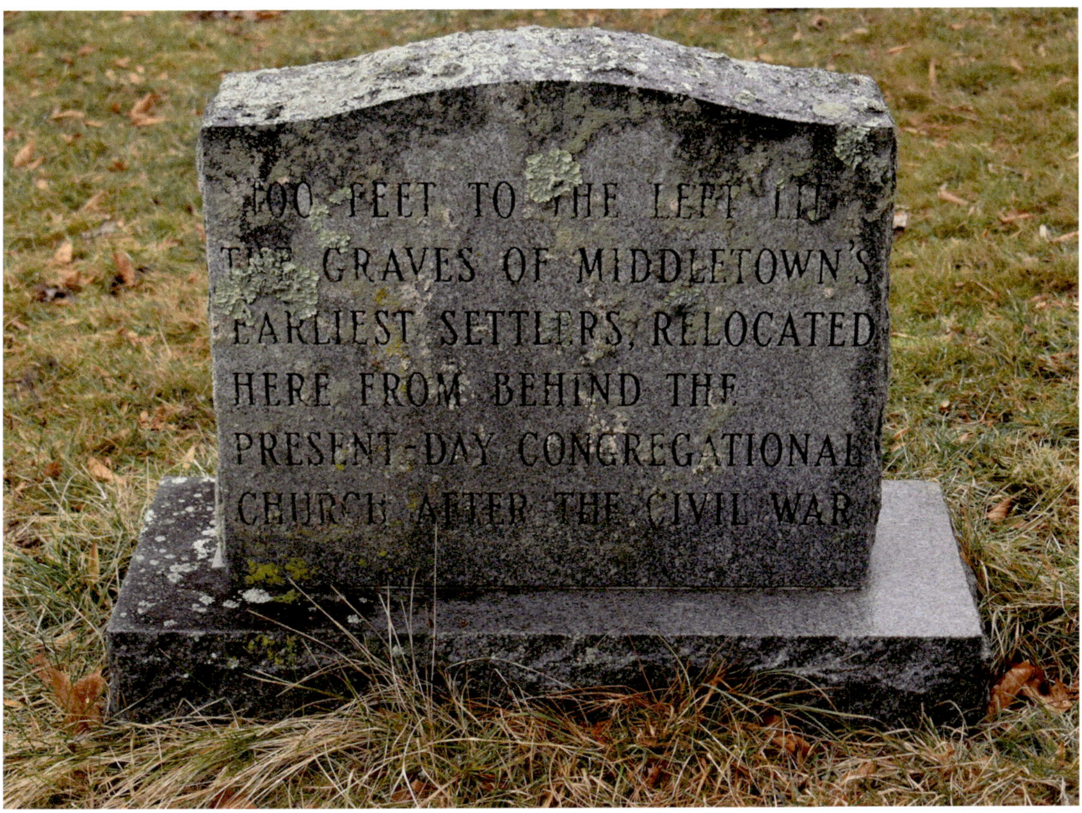

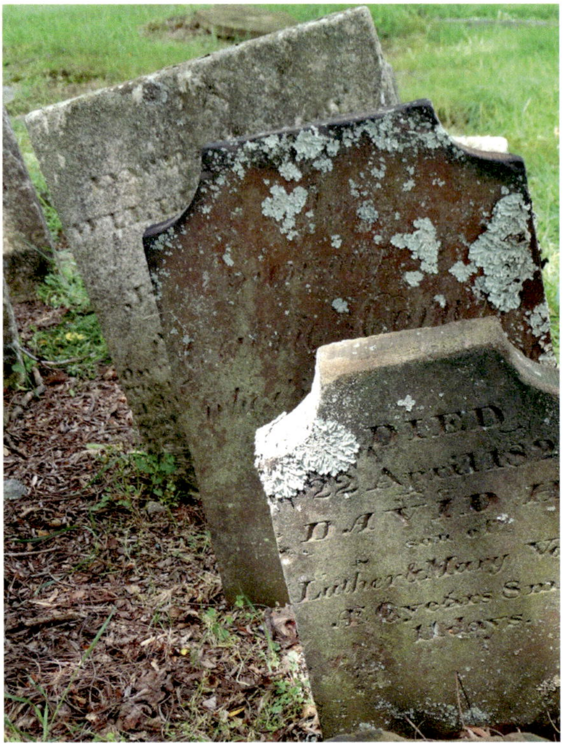

Tombstones that were moved from the Congregational churchyard in 1871 are lined up like dominoes.

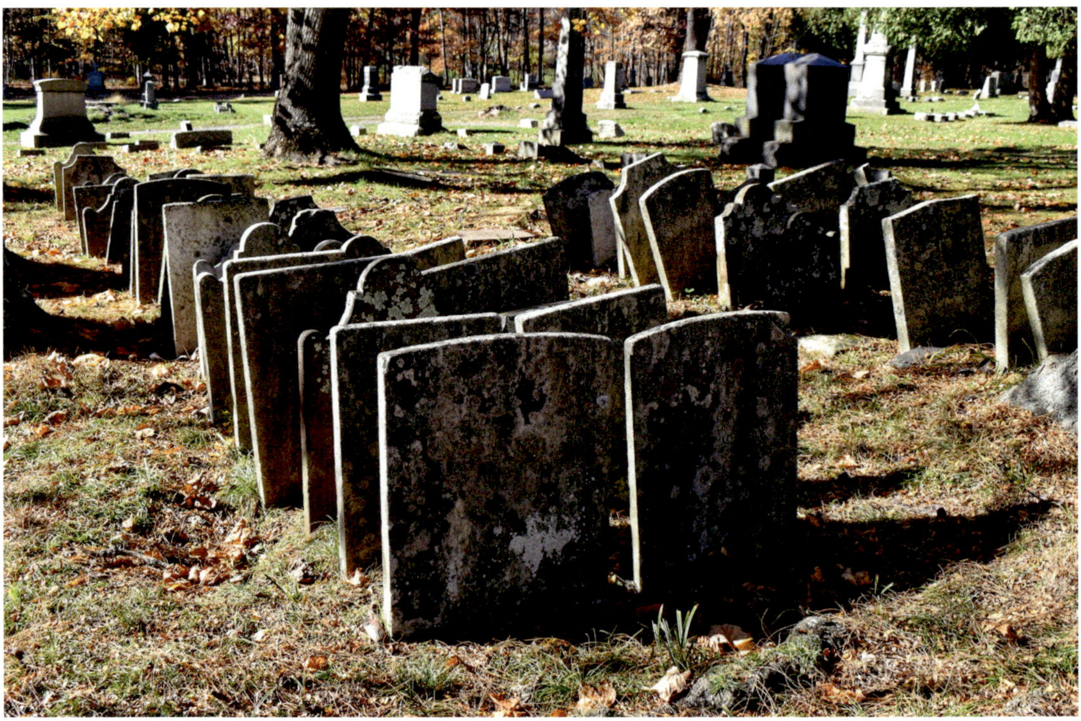

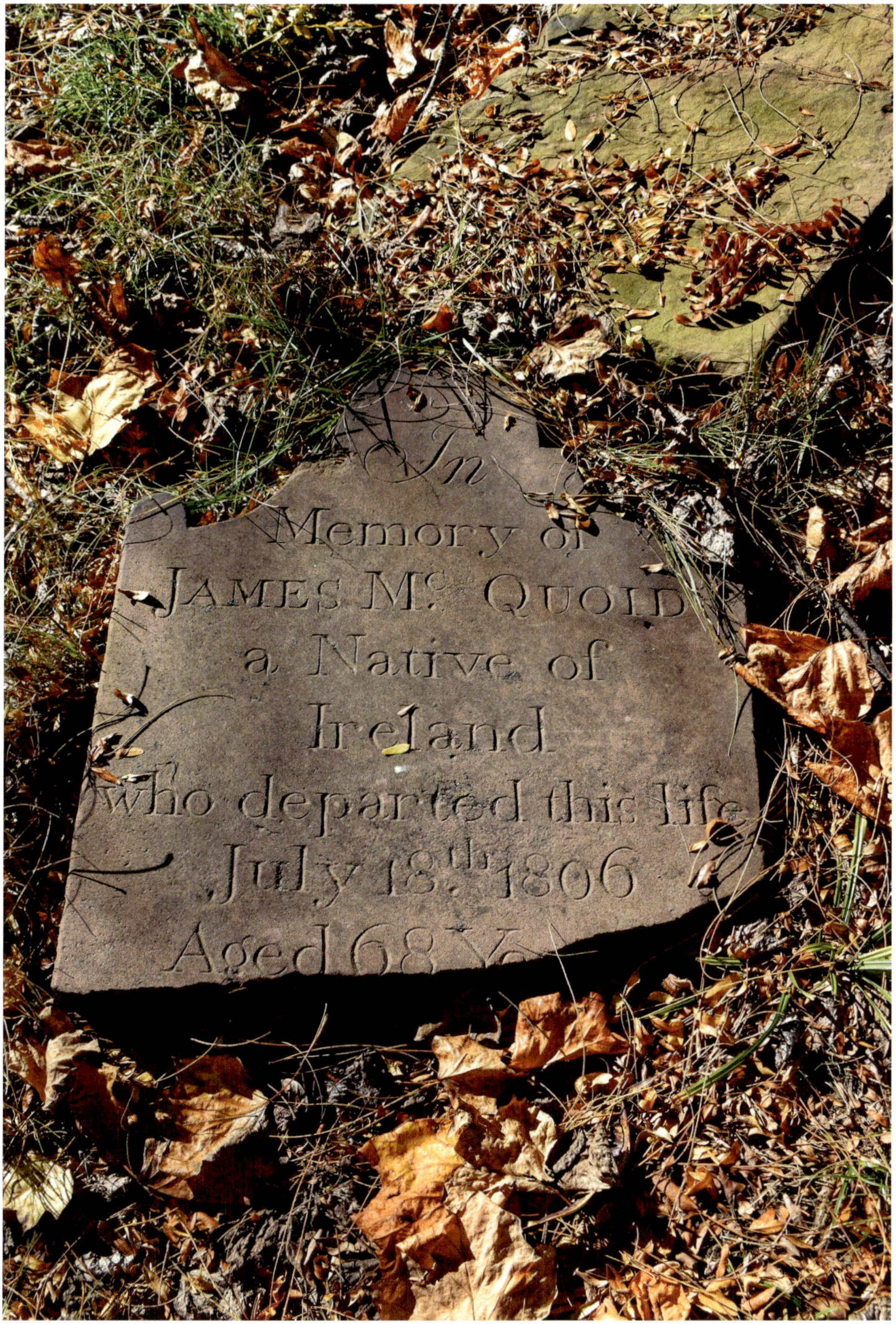

Above and next two pages: Although many of these old stones have been eroded over time, a select few from the churchyard are still legible.

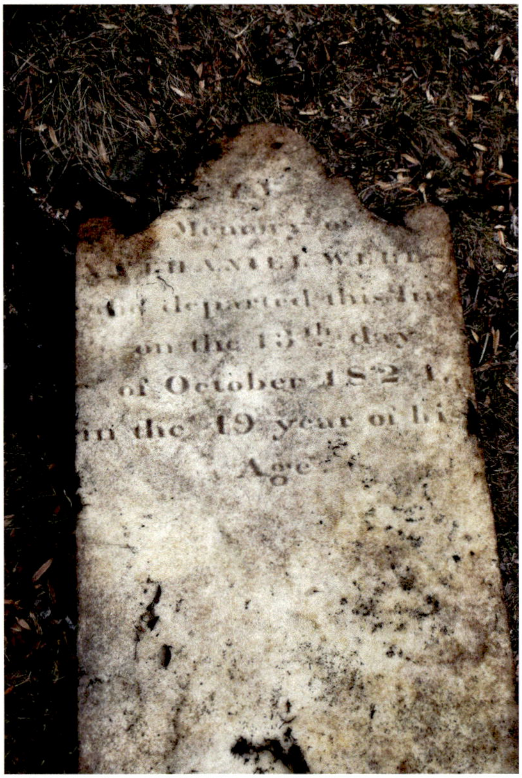
on the 13th day
of October 1824
Age

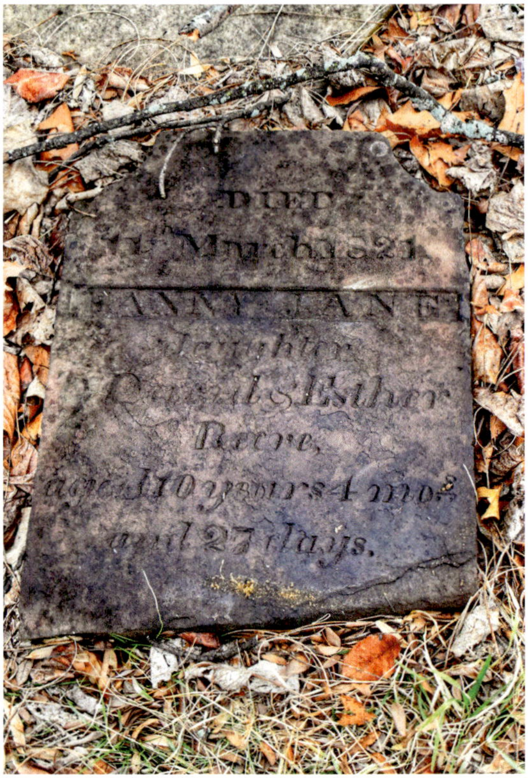
DIED
aged 10 years 4 mos
and 27 days.

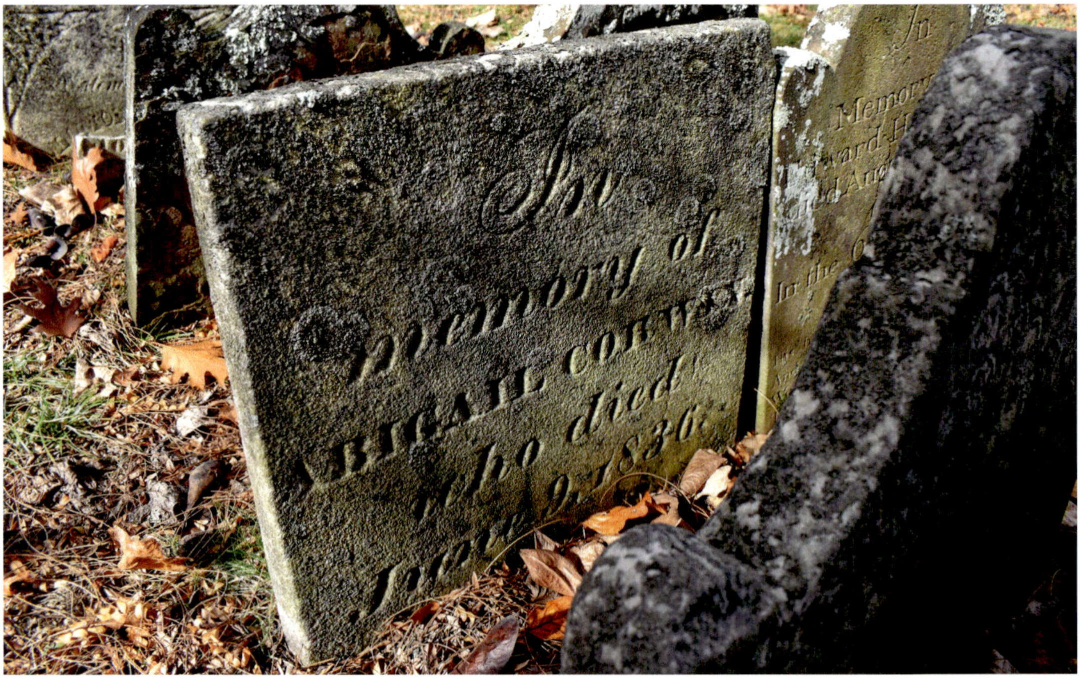
In
Memory of
who died

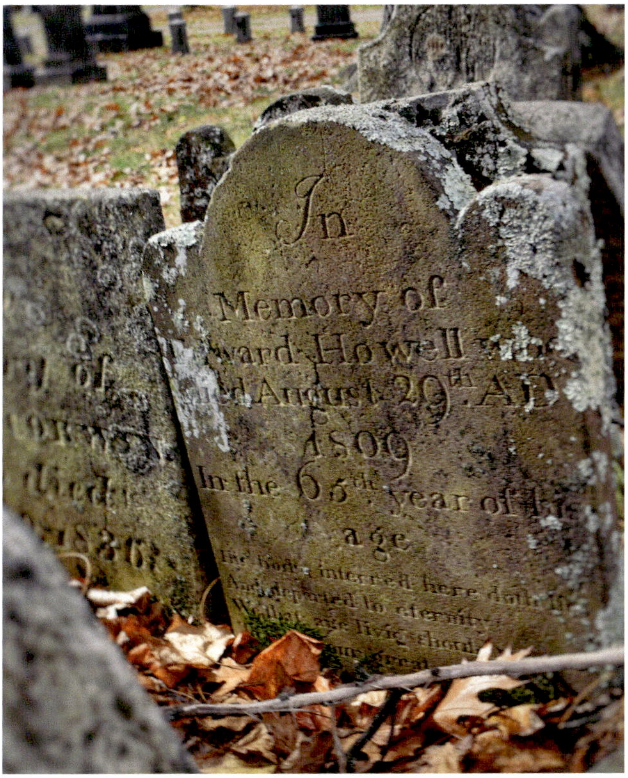
In
Memory of
August 29th AD
1809
In the 65th year of
age

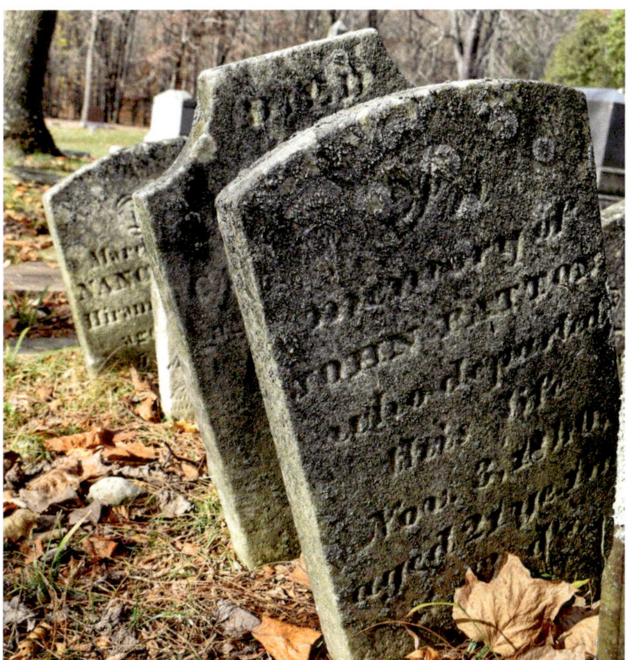

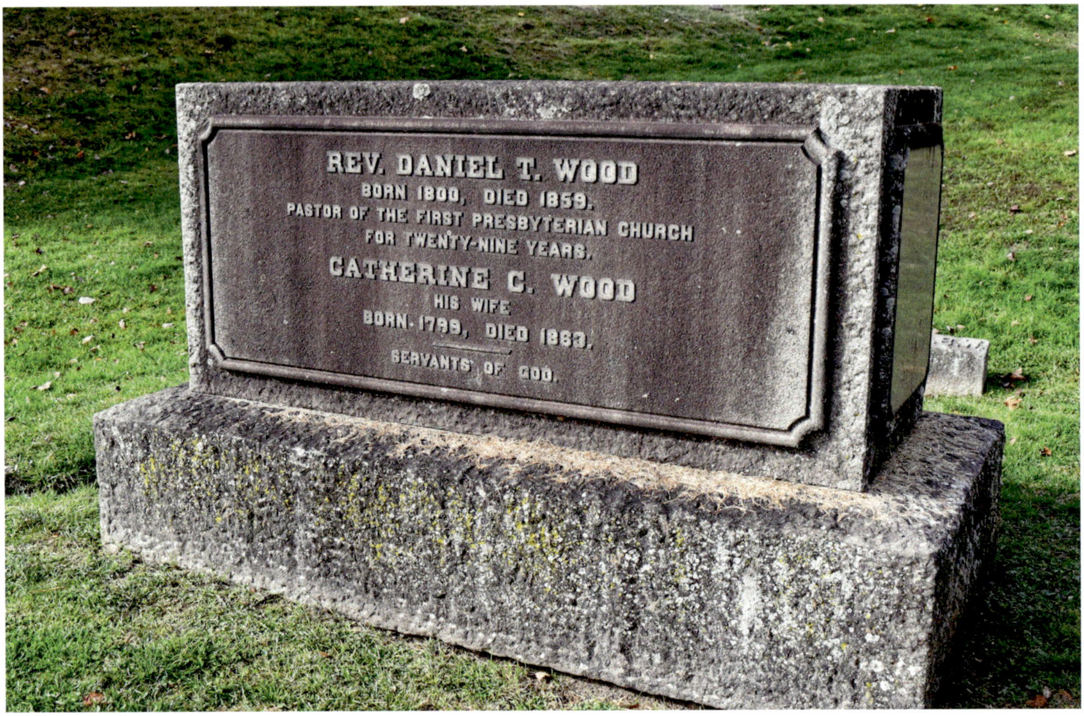

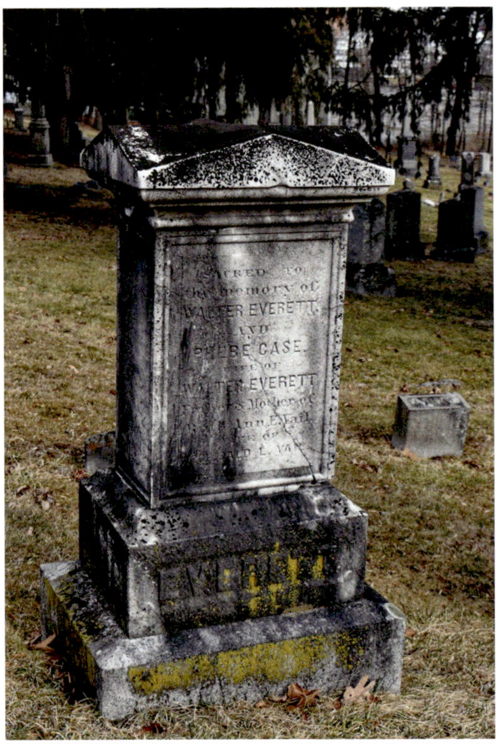

Above: Reverend Daniel T. Wood's grave was relocated from one of the Academy Avenue cemeteries in 1882.

Left: Walter and Phebe Everett were originally buried at Academy Avenue and now have their own plot in Hillside.

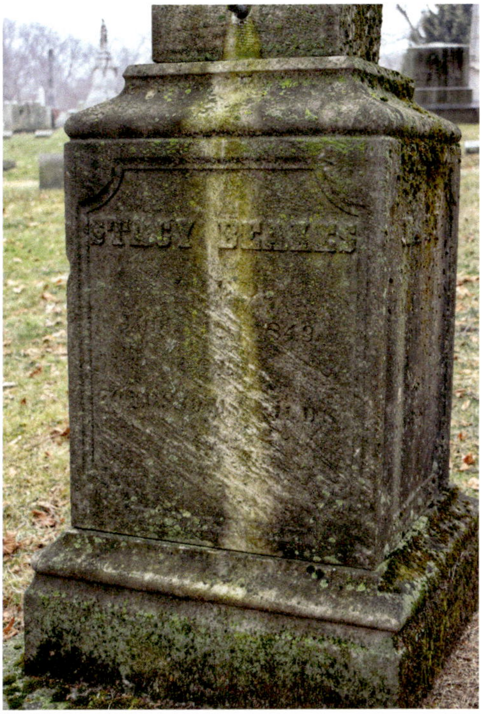

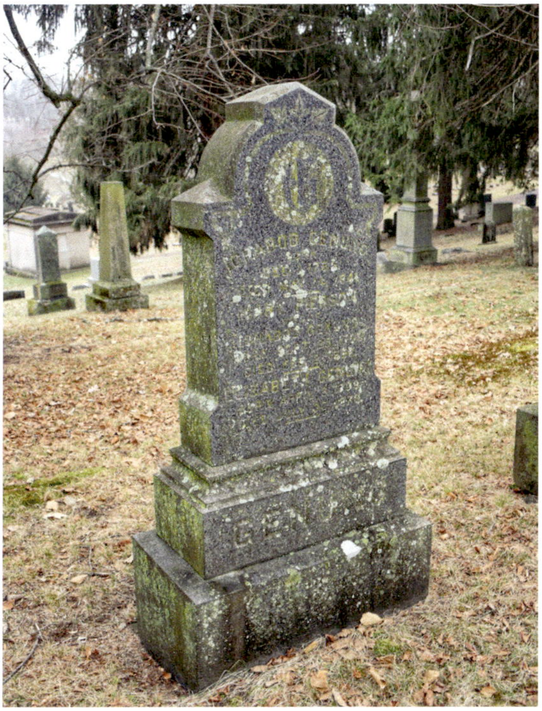

The graves of Stacy Beakes and Ichabod Genung were both relocated from Academy Avenue and are next to each other in Hillside.

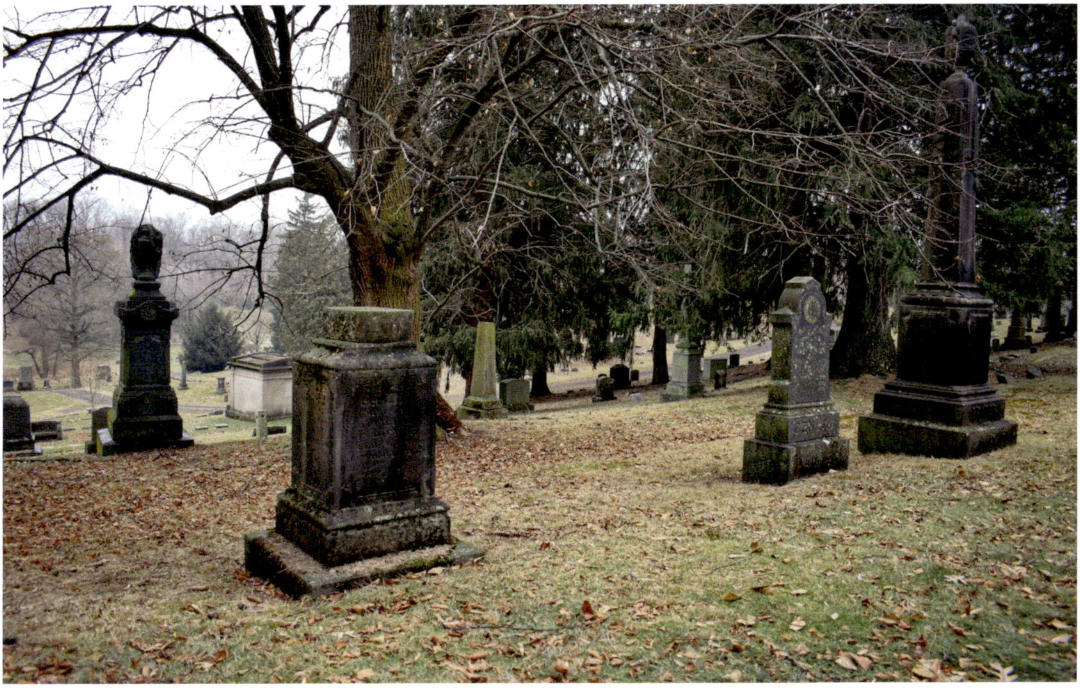

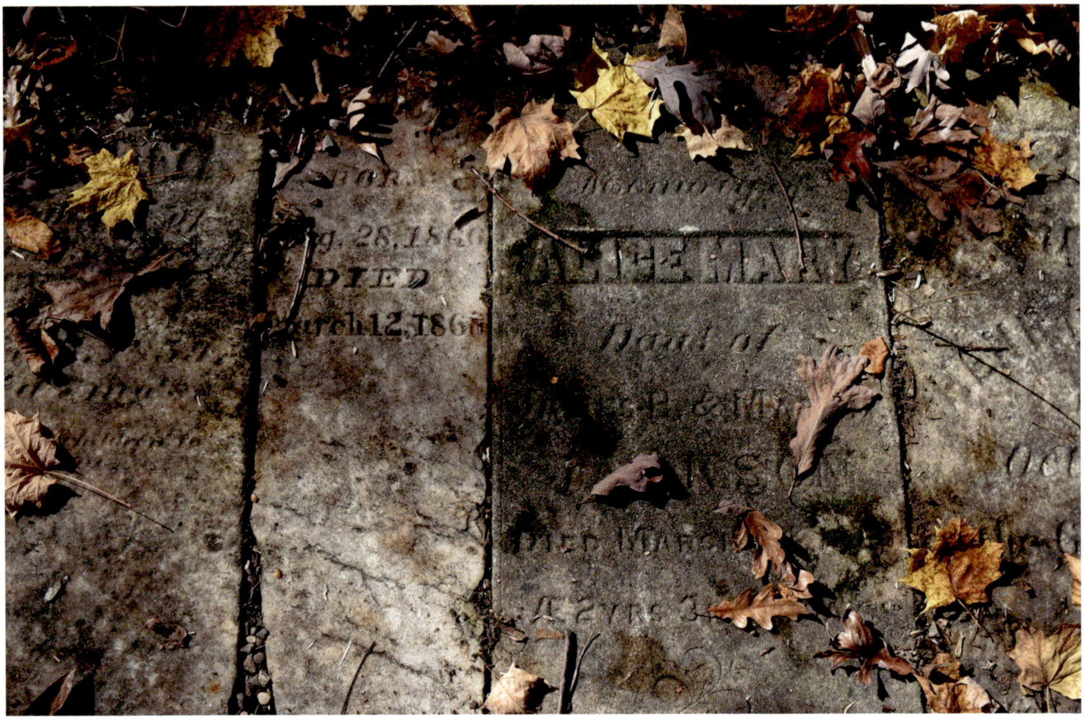

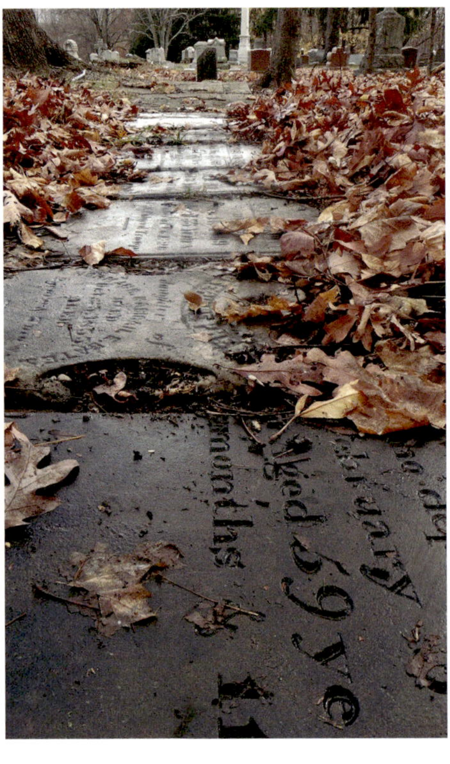

Above ,left and opposite page: Towards the back of the cemetery, the leaf-dappled "walkway" flaunts many beautiful old stones.

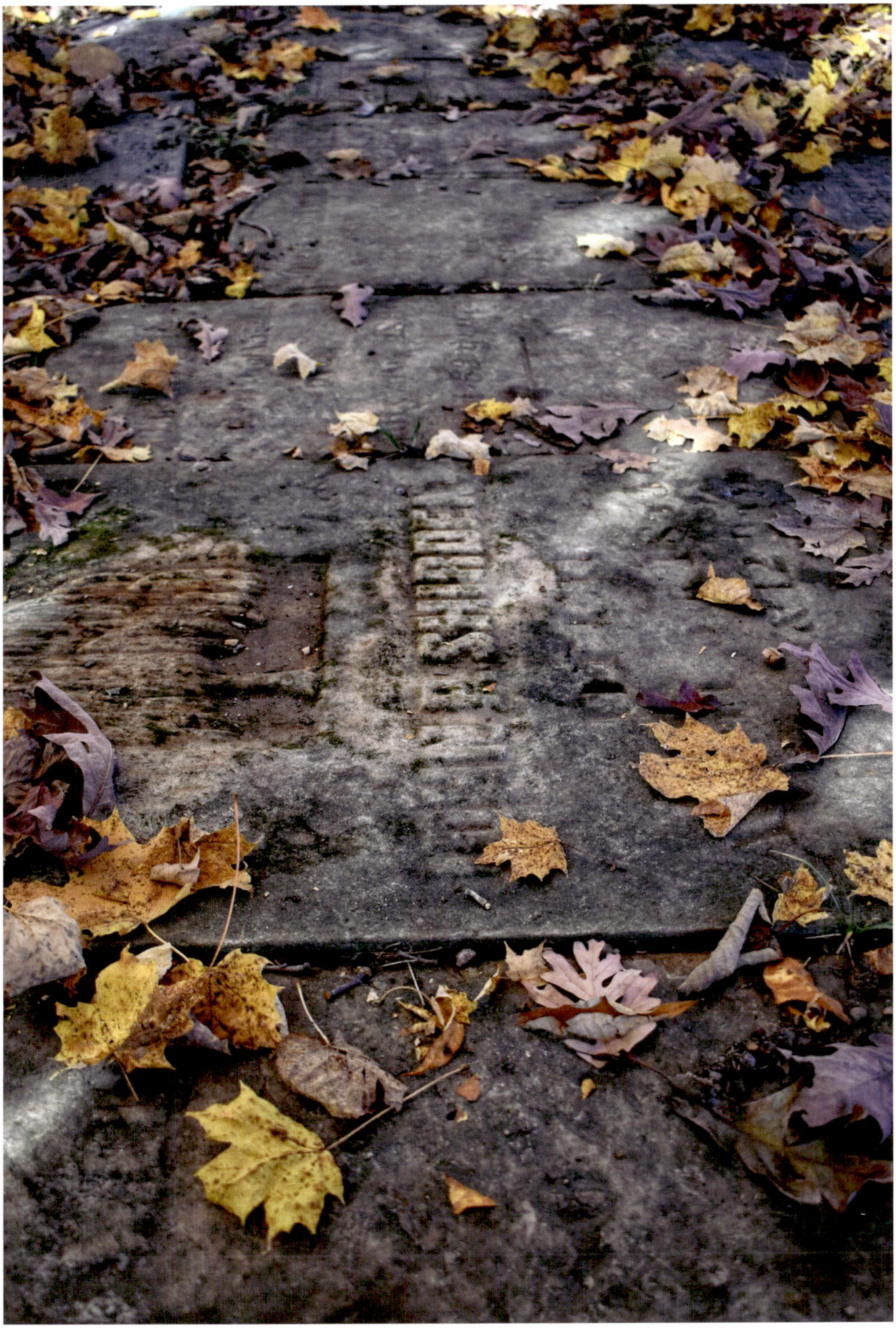

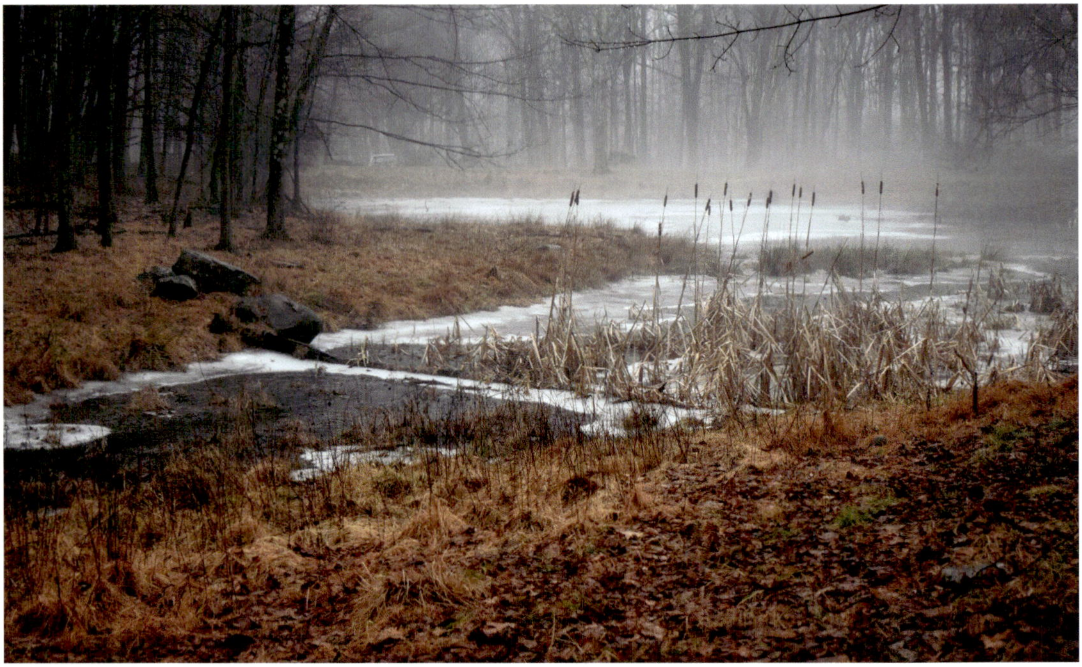

Surrounded by cattails, the former pond is home to turtles, frogs, and an occasional duck.

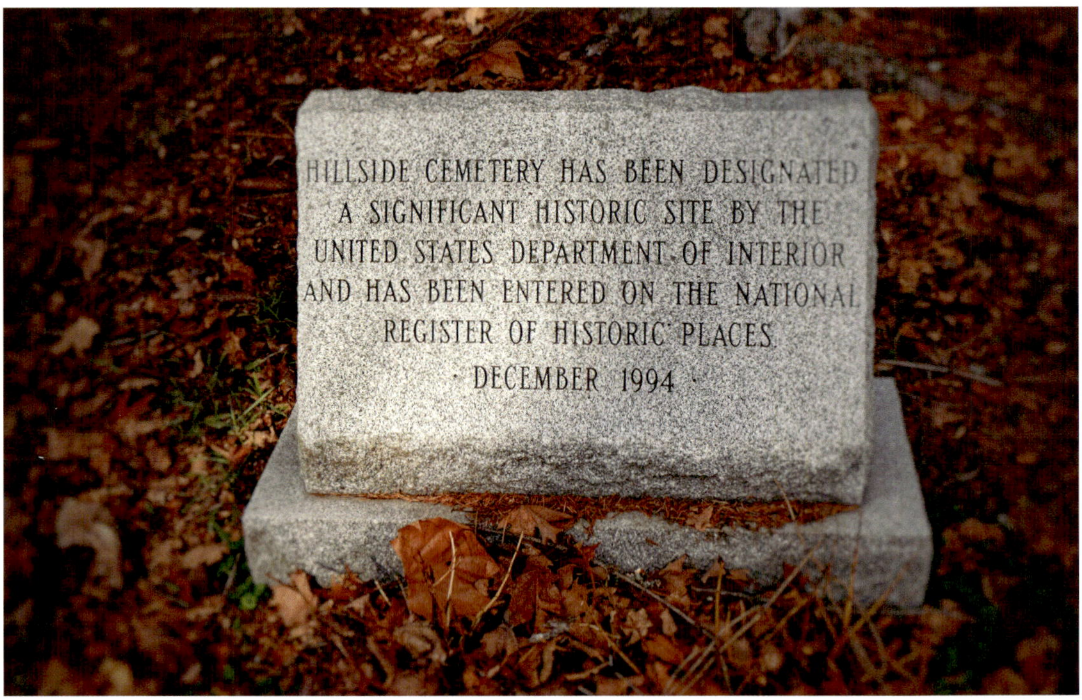

As of 1994, Hillside was nationally designated as a historic place.

2

Notable Doctors of Hillside

Without doctors, communities would cease to exist. Although medicine, cures, and procedures have changed drastically since these men and women practiced, these physicians definitely left their mark in the community.

Dr. David Hanford (1786–1844) arrived in Middletown in 1810. He was the hamlet's first physician. A Yale graduate, Dr. Hanford treated slaves in his earlier days of medical practice, and he often received livestock, vegetables, and other practical goods for his services instead of monetary compensation. Dr. Hanford's treatments included bloodletting and other primitive practices that are obsolete today. His large gravestone sits prominently on the crest of a peaceful hill.

Dr. John B. McMunn (1801–1869) was Middletown's second physician. In the 1830s, he developed "McMunn's Elixir of Opium," which was marketed as a miracle cure-all. Dr. McMunn sold his elixir to a major drug company in 1841; unfortunately, the tonic proved to be fatal in some cases, as some children were overdosed. Medicines like this were not uncommon because rules and regulations were not in place like they are today. Although he was initially buried in Hillside when he died in 1869, Dr. McMunn's grave will not be found there today. For reasons unknown, his remains were relocated in 1889 to Laurel Grove Cemetery in Port Jervis, New York, about twenty miles away.

Dr. Harvey Everett (1811–1899) was Middletown's third physician but the first one to open a pharmacy in 1834. Dr. Everett was the great grandson of David Moore Sr., one of Middletown's first settlers, who arrived here around 1756. The drug store had an oyster bar in the basement. Dr. Everett's family mausoleum is visible upon first entering the cemetery.

Dr. Ira S. Bradner (1820–1894) was a Princeton graduate who became interested in homeopathic (holistic) medicine in the early 1850s. He opened a practice in Middletown around 1857, becoming the first homeopathic physician in town. Dr. Bradner took an active role in the county's own Homeopathic Medical Society. In 1863, he was appointed as an assistant surgeon on the battlefields of the Civil War. Dr. Bradner died as one of the oldest practicing doctors in the county.

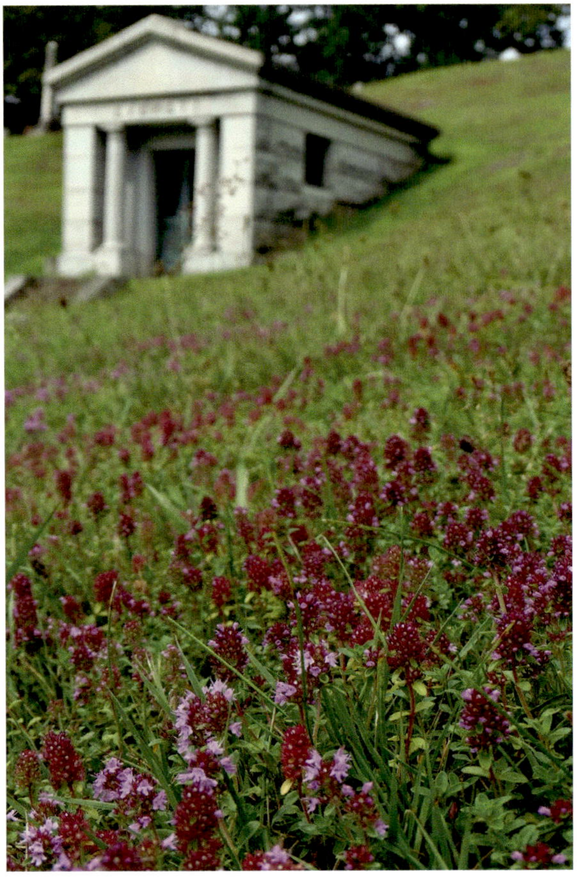

Dr. Harvey Everett's family mausoleum is surrounded by August wildflowers.

Dr. Selden Haynes Talcott (1842–1902) became superintendent of the Middletown State Hospital (then known as "The State Homeopathic Hospital for the Insane at Middletown") in 1877. Dr. Talcott was a respected "alienist" (an outdated term for a psychiatrist). After serving in the Civil War, he graduated in 1872 as valedictorian from the New York Homeopathic College. Dr. Talcott immediately improved conditions for his patients upon his arrival at the state hospital, adding many amenities. He encouraged his employees to treat the patients with kindness, and he believed that mental illness was just as much of a disease as any physical ailment. Dr. Talcott initiated many creative therapies for his patients, including art shows and publication of a newspaper. A baseball team was also created as part of therapy treatment. Known as the Asylums, the team consisted of patients, staff, and semi-professional ball players. The team became popular and a few of the players went on to play professionally, including staff member Jack Chesbro. Chesbro was given his career nickname "Happy Jack" at the Middletown hospital by a patient. Dr. Talcott contributed to significant medical journals and shared his knowledge and insight by giving lectures on mental illness. He ran the hospital for twenty-five years until his sudden death in 1902. He was respected and admired by all; he was truly a man ahead of his time.

Dr. Julia Bradner (1844–1928) was Middletown's first female physician. Following in her father Ira's footsteps, she graduated from the Women's Medical College in 1878. Dr. Bradner launched Middletown's first Home for Aged Women, opened in 1888, and the first hospital, Thrall Hospital, opened in 1892.

Dr. Harvey A. Horton (1832–1861) is buried in Hillside after losing his life on September 4, 1861. Dr. Horton was in Missouri when a passenger train he was riding in was ambushed by Confederate troops. The troops thought that this particular train crossing the Platte River bridge was carrying Union soldiers; they sabotaged the bridge by cutting the timbers and weakening the structure. The 100-passenger train plunged into the river, killing seventeen instantly and wounding the remainder that were on board. Dr. Horton left a wife, Fanny, who was the daughter of noted publisher and Primitive Baptist minister Elder Gilbert Beebe, and an infant daughter, Mary. Mary died in October 1861 and is rumored to be buried with her father. Dr. Horton was said to be a brilliant man and he was expected to achieve greatness in his field had he lived.

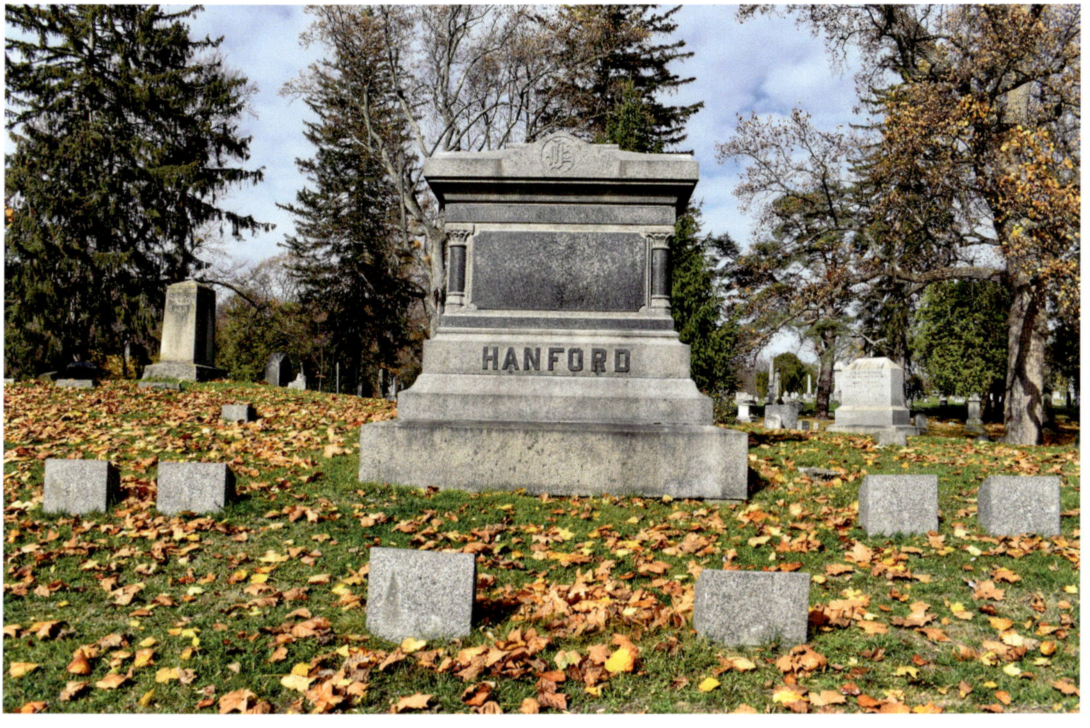

The simple yet stately plot of Dr. David Hanford, Middletown's first physician, rests on a quiet hilltop.

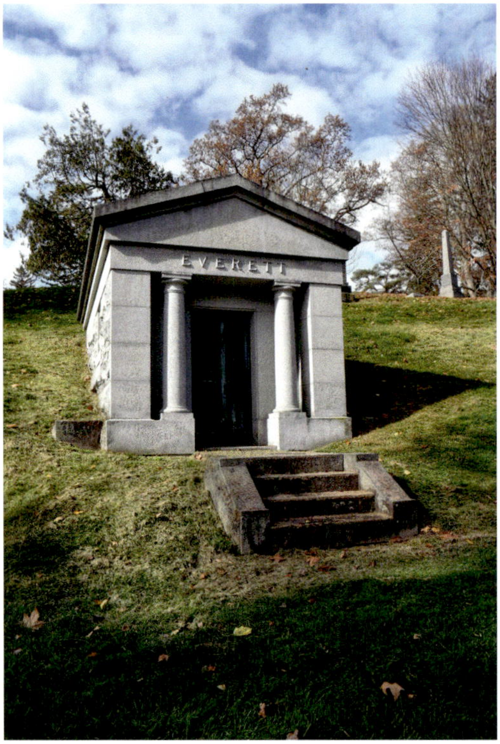

Left: Dr. Harvey Everett, physician and pharmacist, is buried here in the family's mausoleum.

Below: The plain marker of Dr. Ira Bradner is accompanied by a plaque acknowledging his service in the Civil War.

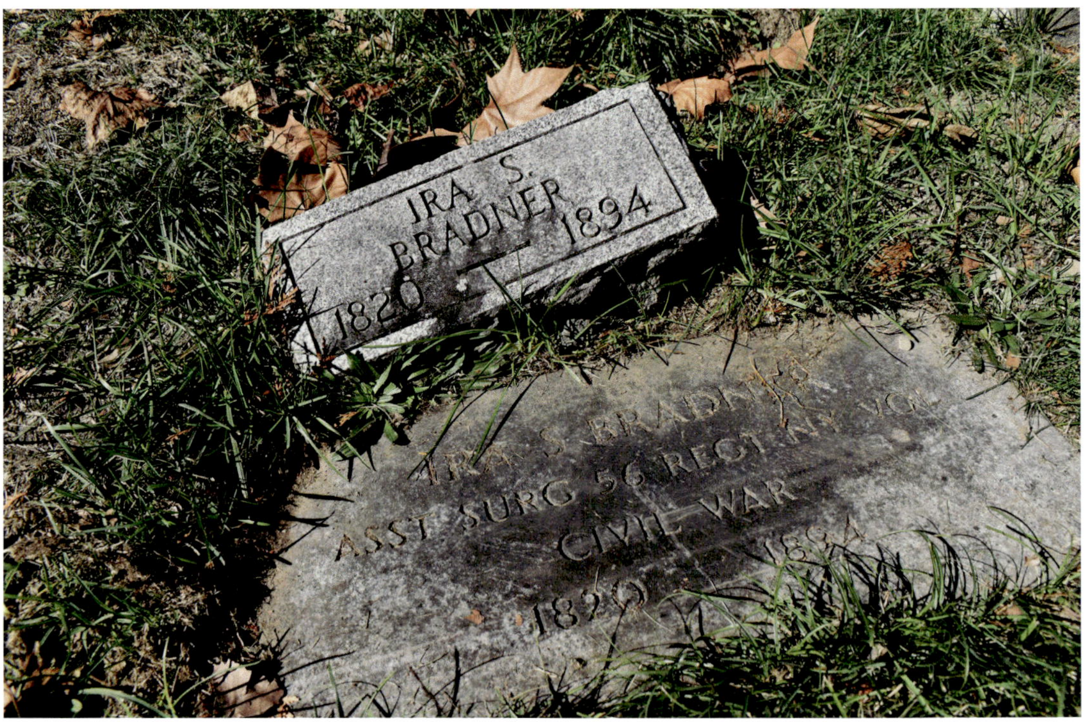

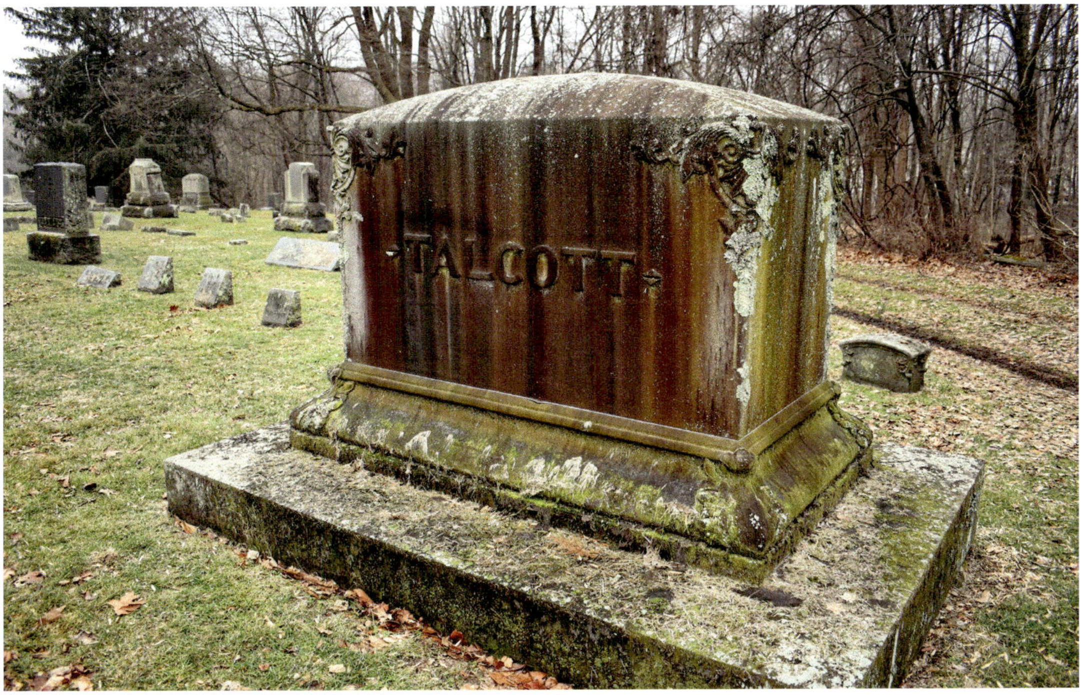

The stones are weathered at Dr. Selden Talcott's grave. Dr. Talcott was an acclaimed "alienist" and was greatly admired by his patients and colleagues.

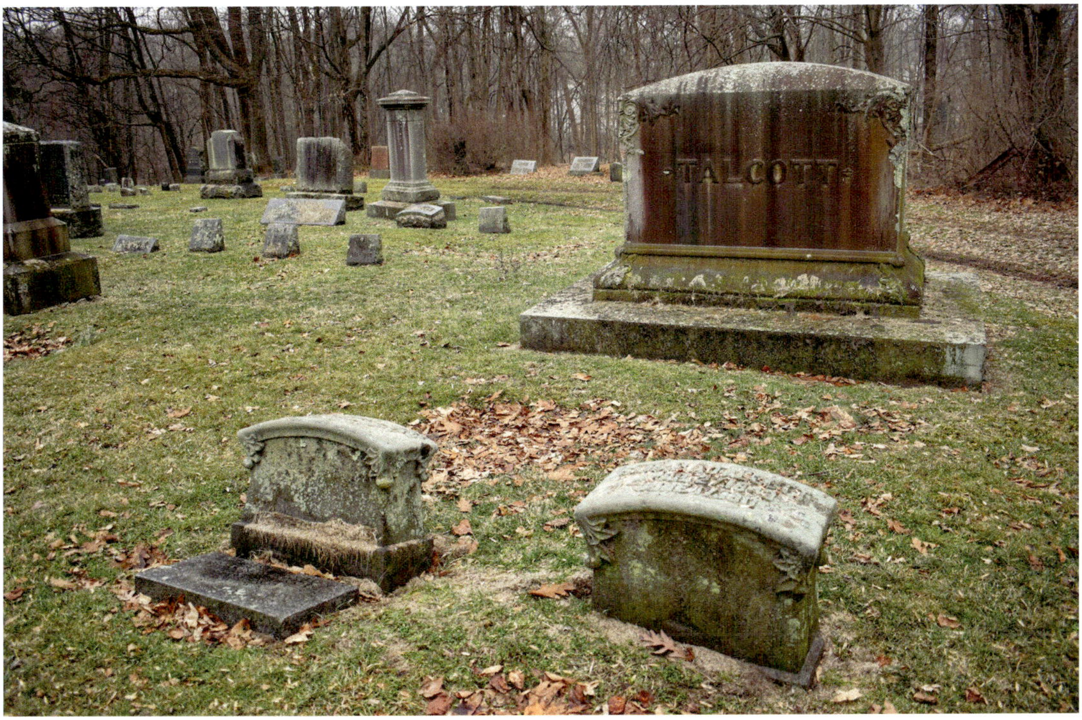

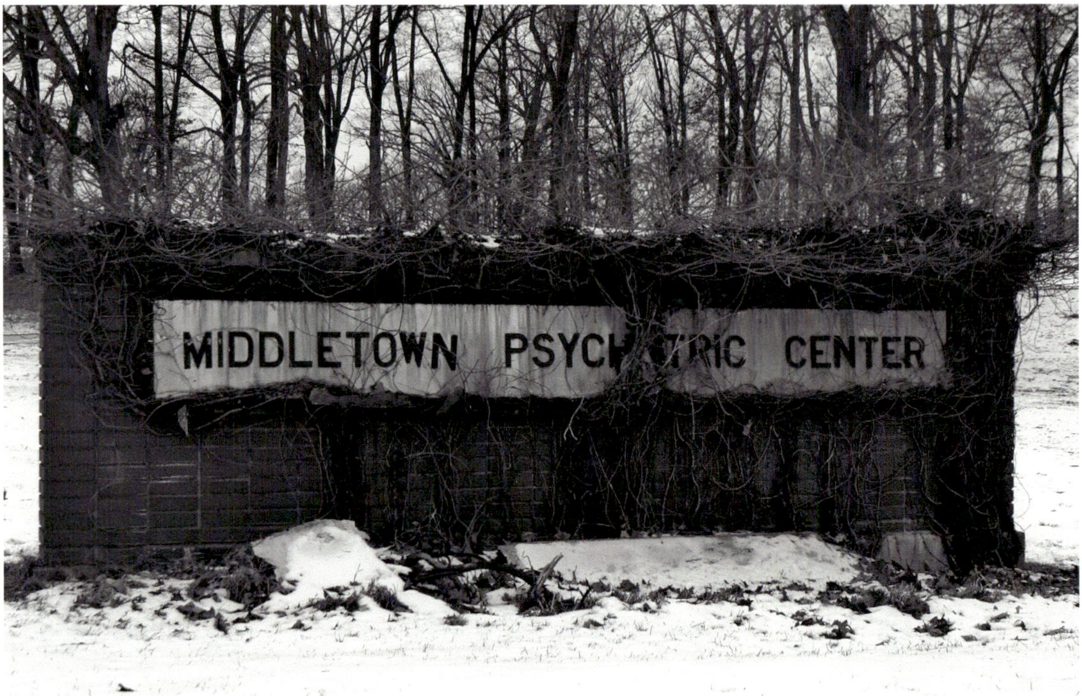

A vine-covered sign marks the entrance to Dr. Talcott's hospital. This particular name change had taken place years after his death.

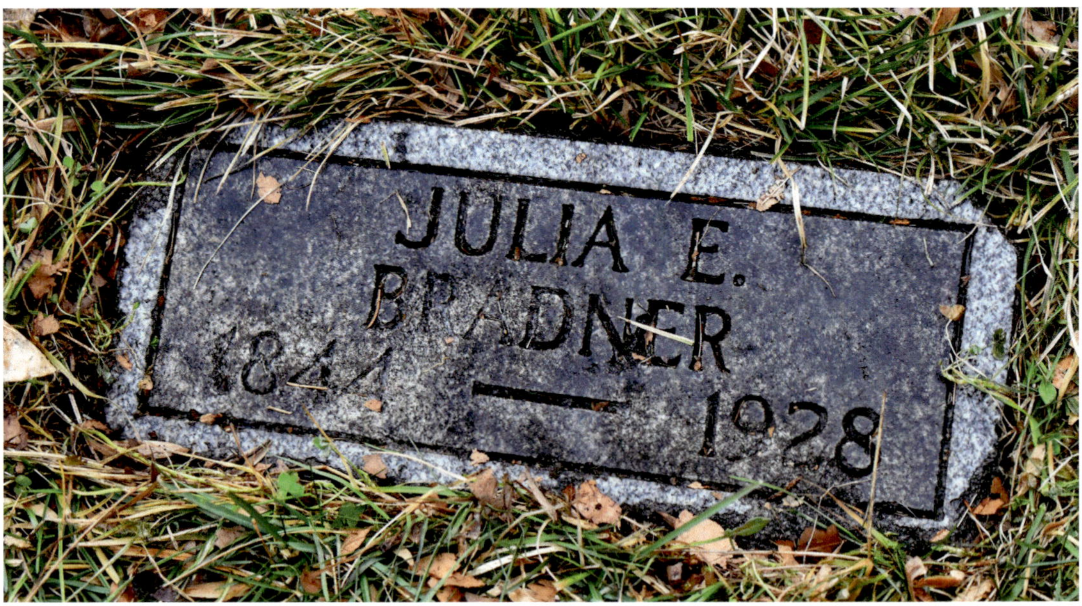

Dr. Julia Bradner, Middletown's first female physician, helped organize the first home for aging ladies and the first hospital in the city.

3

Civil War Heroes of Hillside

Although Hillside contains many war heroes and veterans, there are approximately 200 soldiers buried here that participated in the Civil War. The cemetery has a large soldier's monument honoring these and the other "soldiers, sailors and marines of all wars." These were local boys and men, some who came home after the war to rejoin society, some who came home wounded, and some who came home to rest in Hillside Cemetery. All are heroes.

New York had three units of African American troops, one of them being the 26th Regiment. The USCT (United States Colored Troops) faced a greater danger, as they were treated harsher than white Union troops and were denied medical care if captured. Among them in Hillside are Charles Easterly (1840–1892), Co. F, 26th, and Richard Abbott (1822–1869), Co. E, 26th. Edmund Colden (1823–1877), Co. I, 14th, Rhode Island, was also a soldier in the USCT and his stone lies flat on the walkway section at the back of Hillside Cemetery.

The 124th Regiment, also known as the "Orange Blossoms," were volunteers from Orange County, New York, that enlisted to fight in the Civil War. The troops engaged in major battles, including Chancellorsville and Gettysburg.

Henry Dill (1833–1899), 124th, enlisted in 1862. He was wounded and captured in 1864, paroled in 1865, and discharged from service for his disability. Sadly, he died at the state hospital in 1899. For years, Dill's grave was considered lost. Although the bottom portion is missing, it has since been recovered and is lying in a hilly, wooded area on the back edge of the cemetery.

Adam Beakes (1844–1921), 124th, was wounded in the Battle of Chancellorsville in May 1863. His arm was hit by a bullet and had to be amputated in one of the field hospitals. Beakes came home with a missing limb and went on to become town supervisor for three terms; in 1895, he took on the duties of sheriff.

Egbert Puff (1842–1900), 124th, was also wounded at Chancellorsville and came home as an amputee.

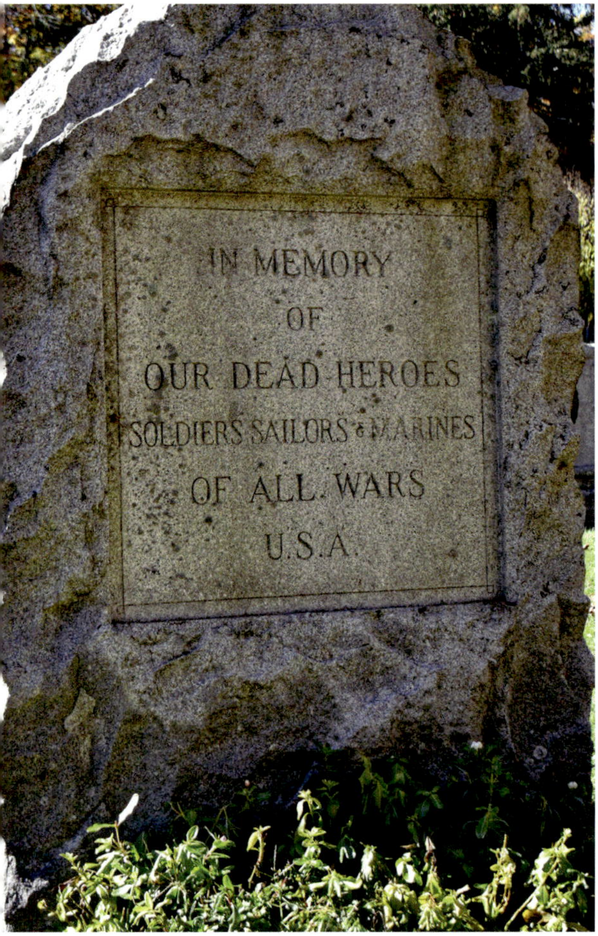

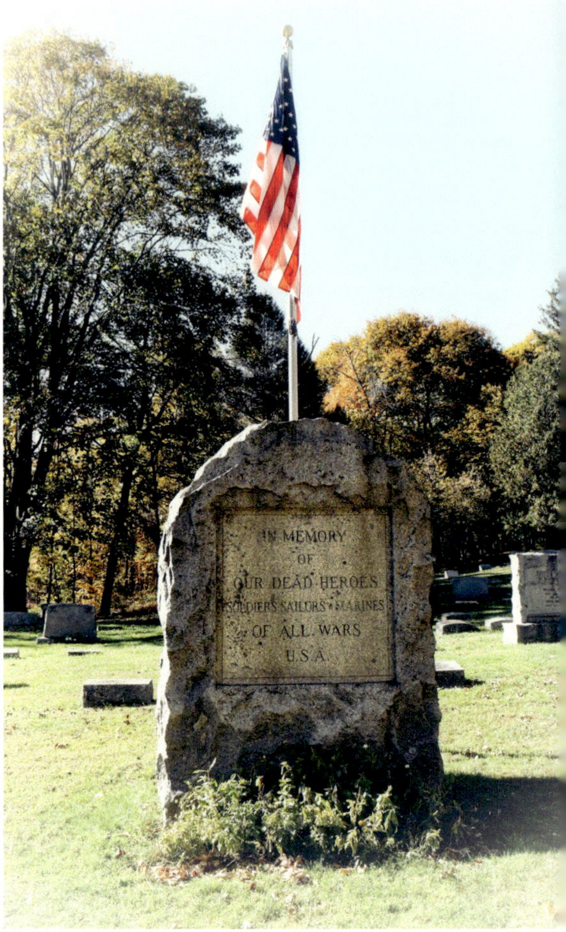

The soldier's monument in Hillside honors the fallen veterans of all wars.

Daniel Webb (1842–1863), 124th, was wounded and captured at Chancellorsville, in early May 1863. He was paroled May 14 only to succumb to his injuries at a Virginia hospital in August.

Gabriel Tuthill (d. 1898), 124th, was a Lieutenant in Company B. He was injured not during the war, but years later. He was a traveling salesman and received spinal injuries in 1891 from a railroad accident in Long Island. The railroad company awarded him $18,000 for his pain and suffering, although Tuthill spent the money touring the country. He died in the state hospital in 1898, penniless. His grave is listed as missing.

There are three Medal of Honor Recipients buried in Hillside, two of them belonging to the 124th.

Nathan M Hallock (1844–1903), 124th, was a banker before and after the war. He received his Medal of Honor for carrying a disabled officer to safety June 1863, in Bristoe Station, Virginia.

Lewis Wisner (1841–1906), 124th, exposed himself to enemy fire in Spotsylvania, Virginia, May 1864. He was unscathed, but his uniform was riddled with bullet holes. Capt. Wisner received a Medal of Honor for his heroic deeds that day. Sadly, in 1906, while in a cattle pen at his farm, he was gored by one of his bulls. Capt. Wisner died from his injuries four days later.

Although not a member of the Orange Blossoms, Sgt. Thomas Collins (1847–1935), of Co. H, 143rd, received his Medal of Honor for capturing an enemy flag in Resaca, Georgia, in May 1864. His grave is near the soldier's monument.

Other notable soldiers in Hillside include Capt. G.A. Webb (d. 1865), 127th, who was killed in action; Abner S. Wells (1838–1919), originally part of the "Middletown Calvary", Co. C, 1st Mounted Rifles, N.Y.; and Civil War Union Brevet Brigadier General David Porter DeWitt (1817–1889). Gen. DeWitt graduated from West Point, fourteenth in his class, in 1836. He became a civil engineer to construct railroads. In 1861, he entered the Union Army. In 1865, he was brevetted Brigadier General, an honorary promotion for his loyal service and valor during the war.

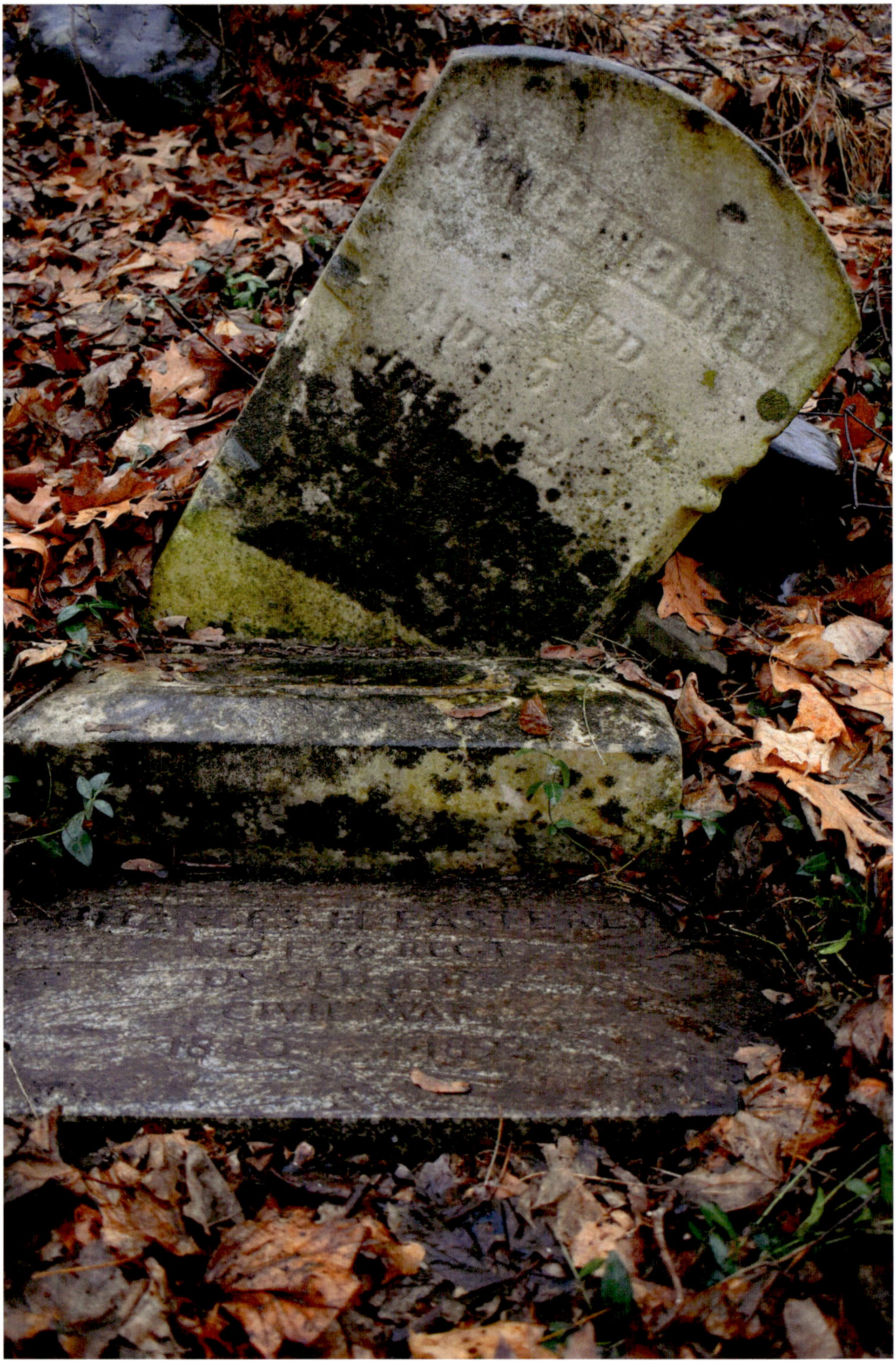

USCT soldier Charles Easterly's grave sits in a forgotten corner at the back of Hillside.

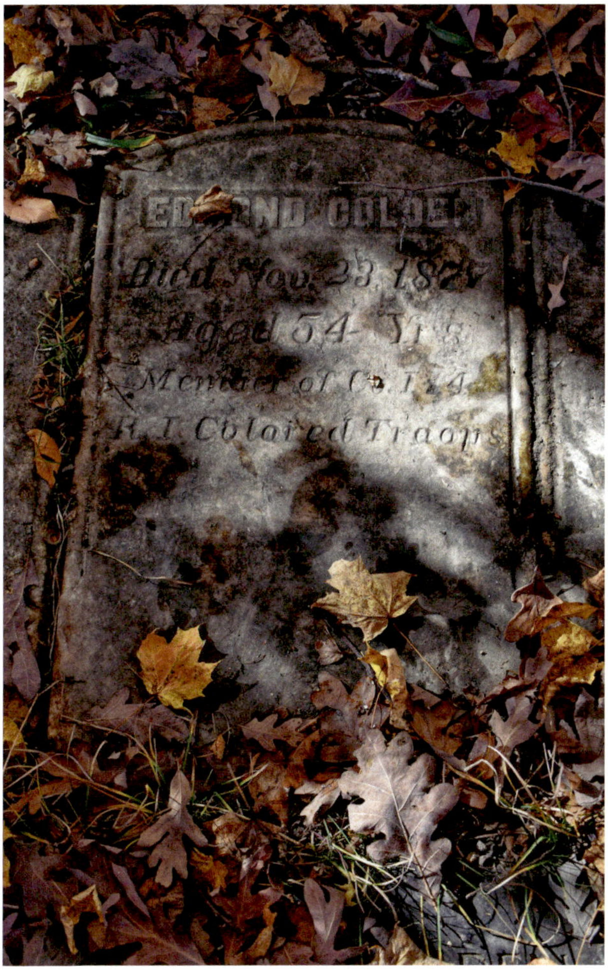

USCT soldiers Edmund Colden, Richard Abbott, and John Roberts have stones lying along the walkway section of the cemetery.

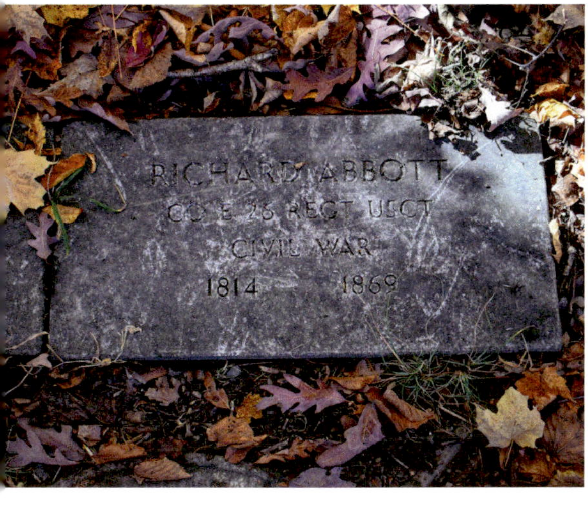

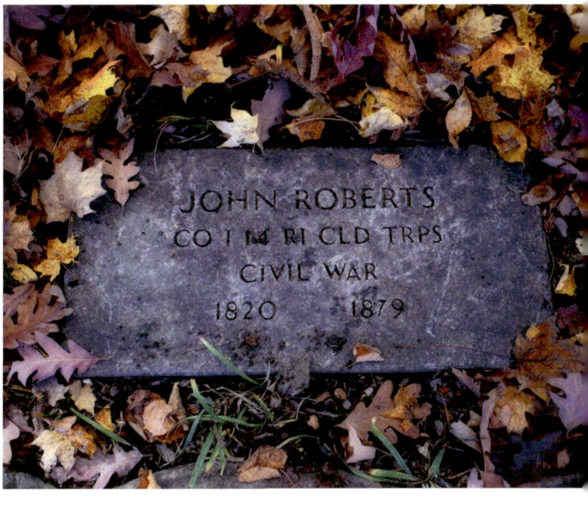

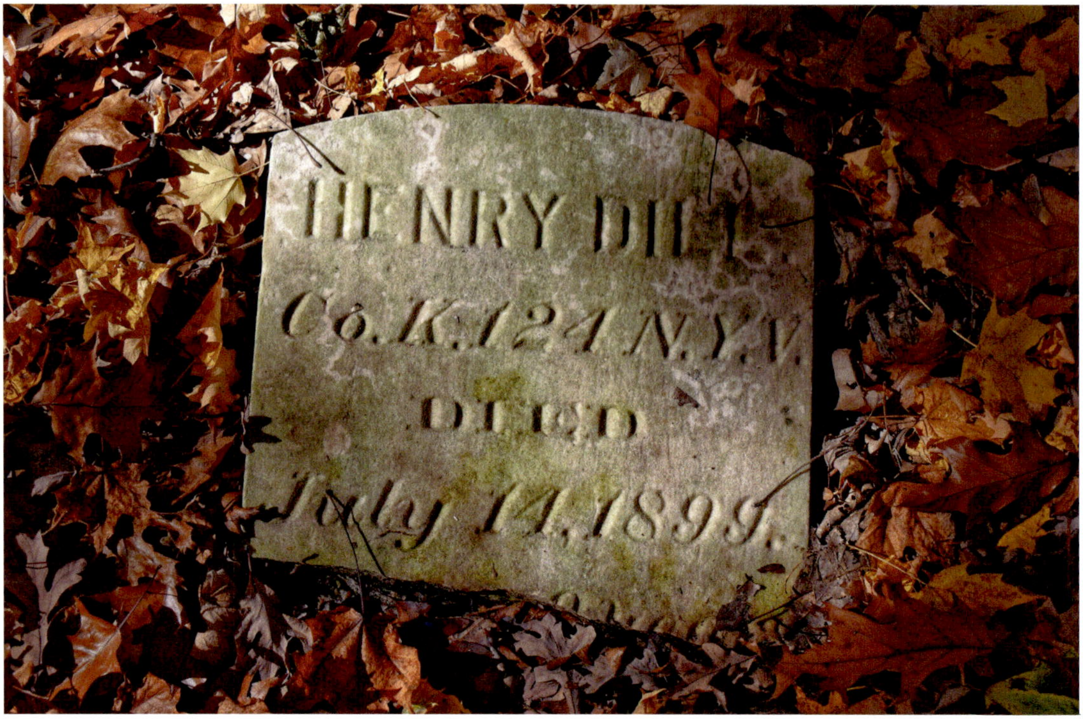

Henry Dill was an "Orange Blossom." His grave was lost for many years.

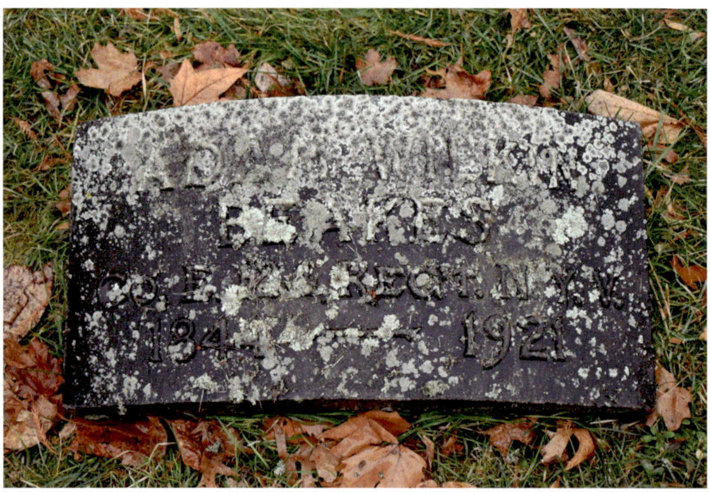

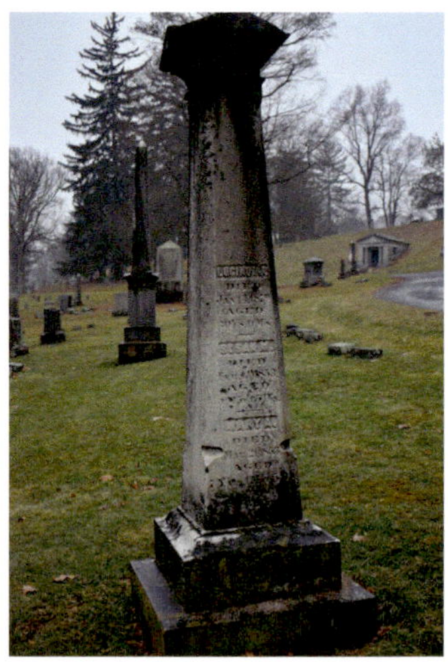

The Adam W. Beakes family plot. Beakes, also an "Orange Blossom," came home an amputee and then became a sheriff.

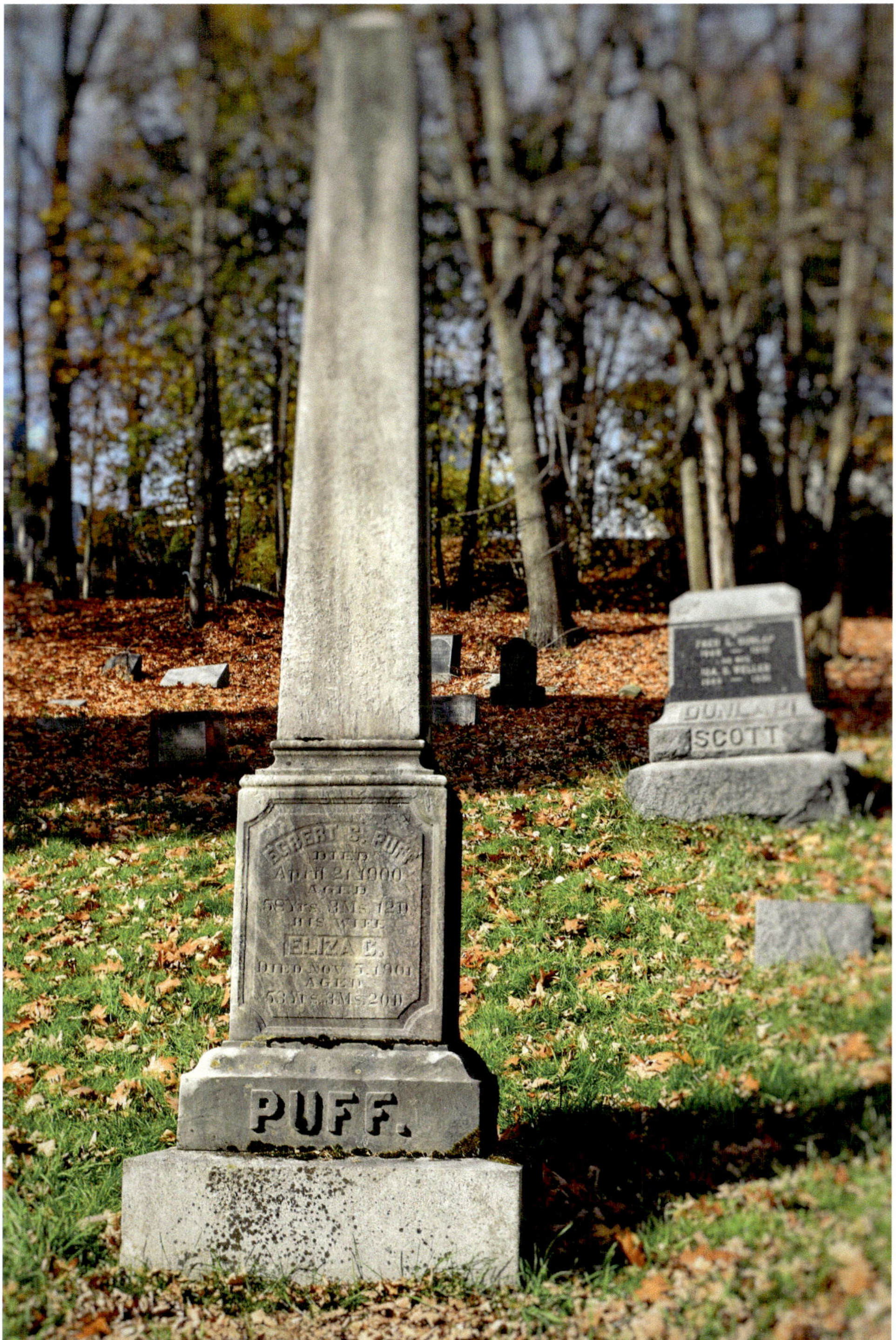

Egbert Puff was wounded in the same battle as Beakes and also came home as an amputee.

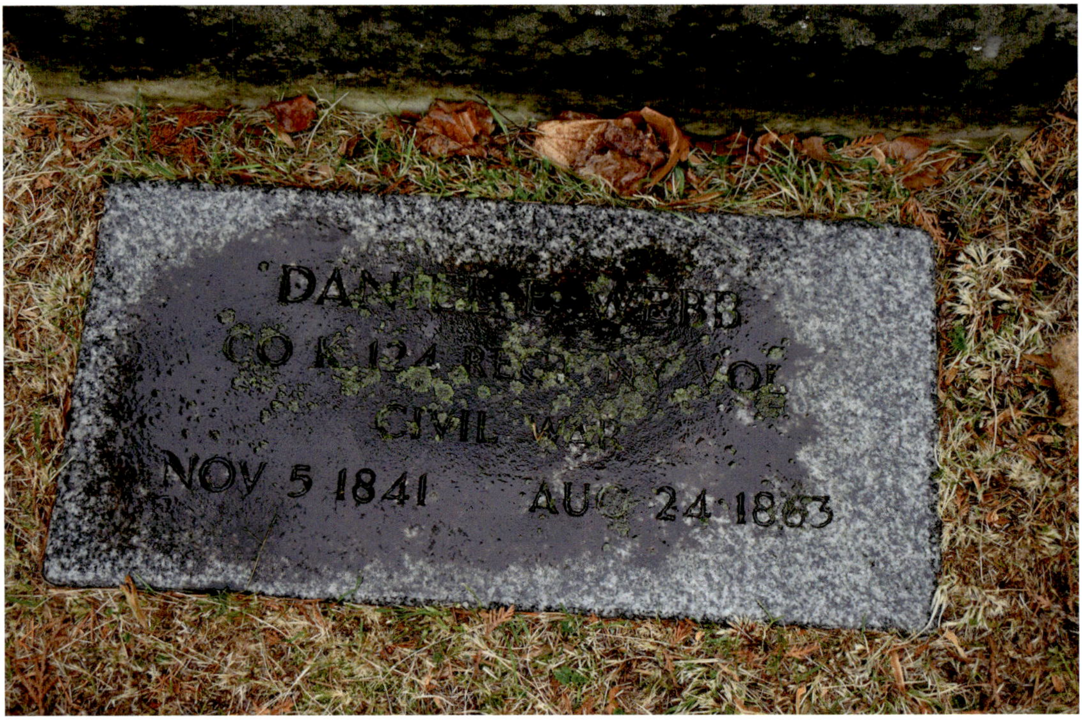

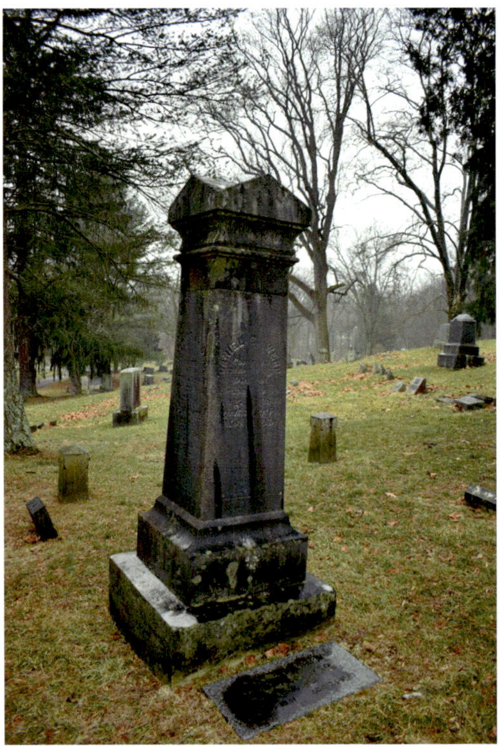

The Webb family plot is where Daniel is interred. Daniel was wounded in battle and died a few months later in Virginia.

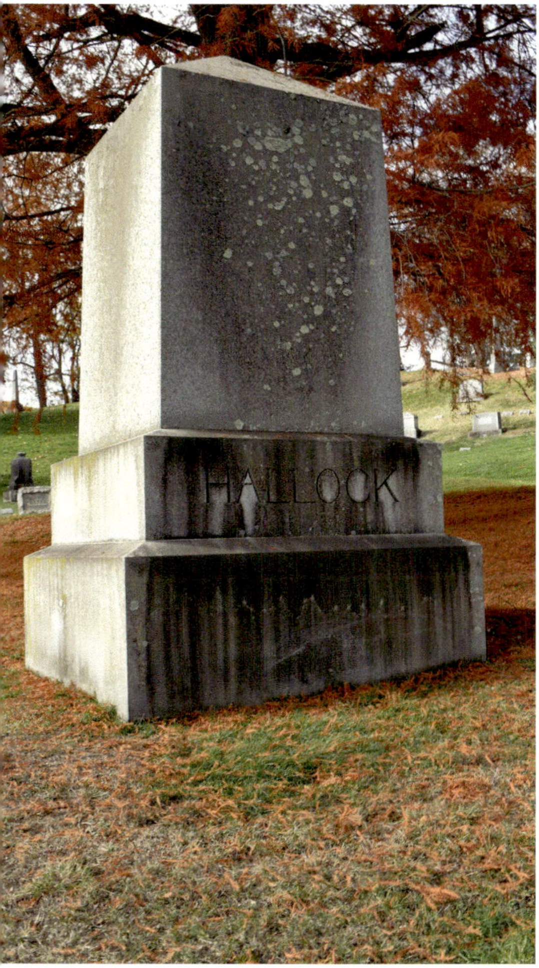

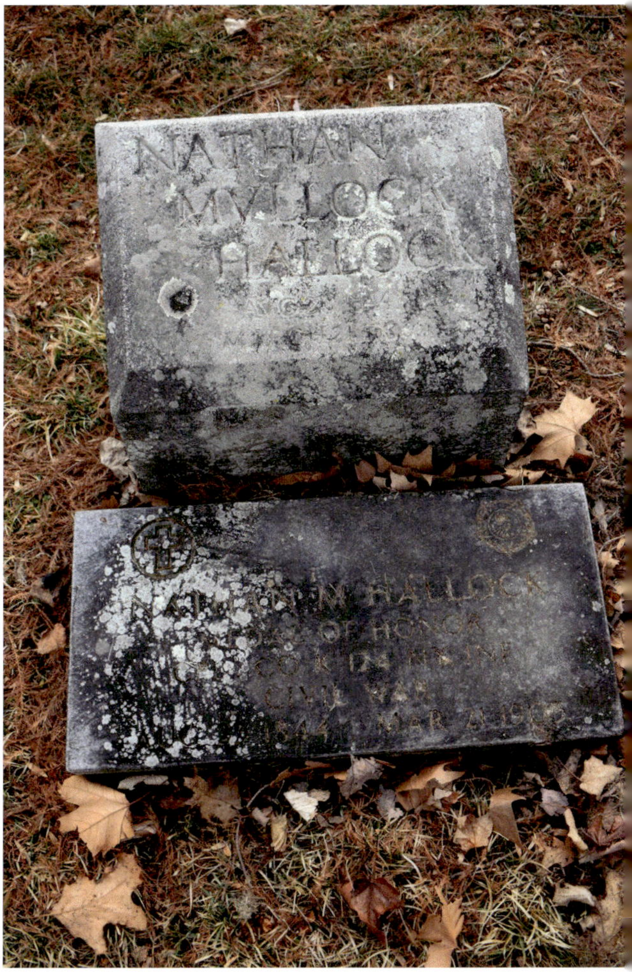

Nathan M. Hallock received a Medal of Honor for his bravery during the war.

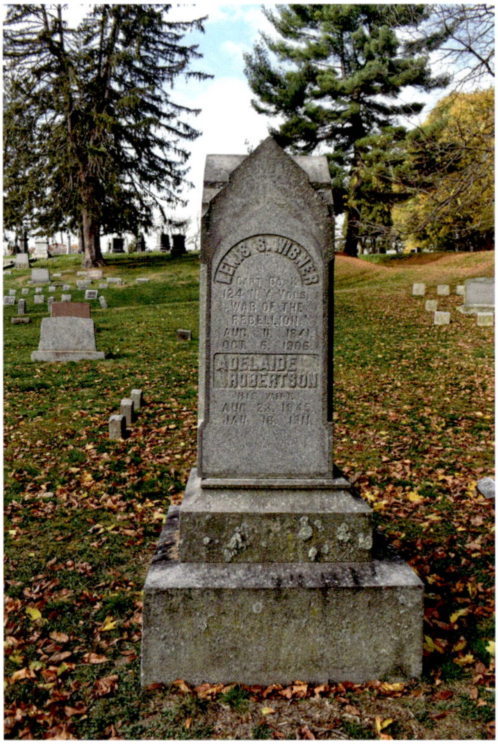

The Wisner plot is where Capt. Lewis Wisner, Medal of Honor recipient, is buried.

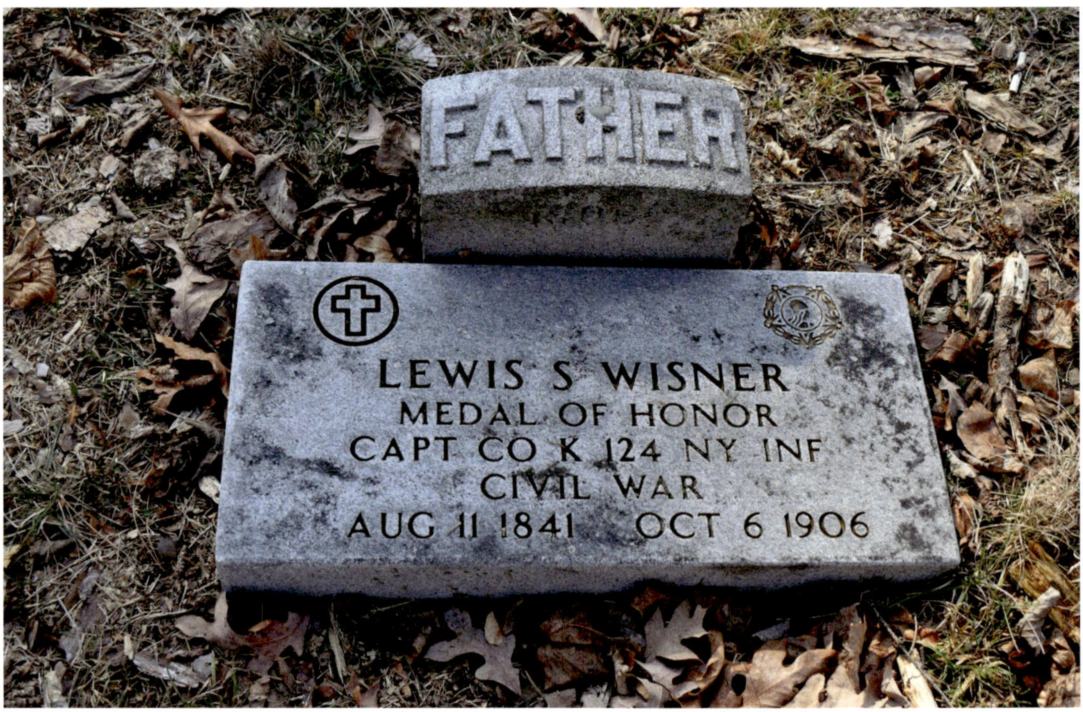

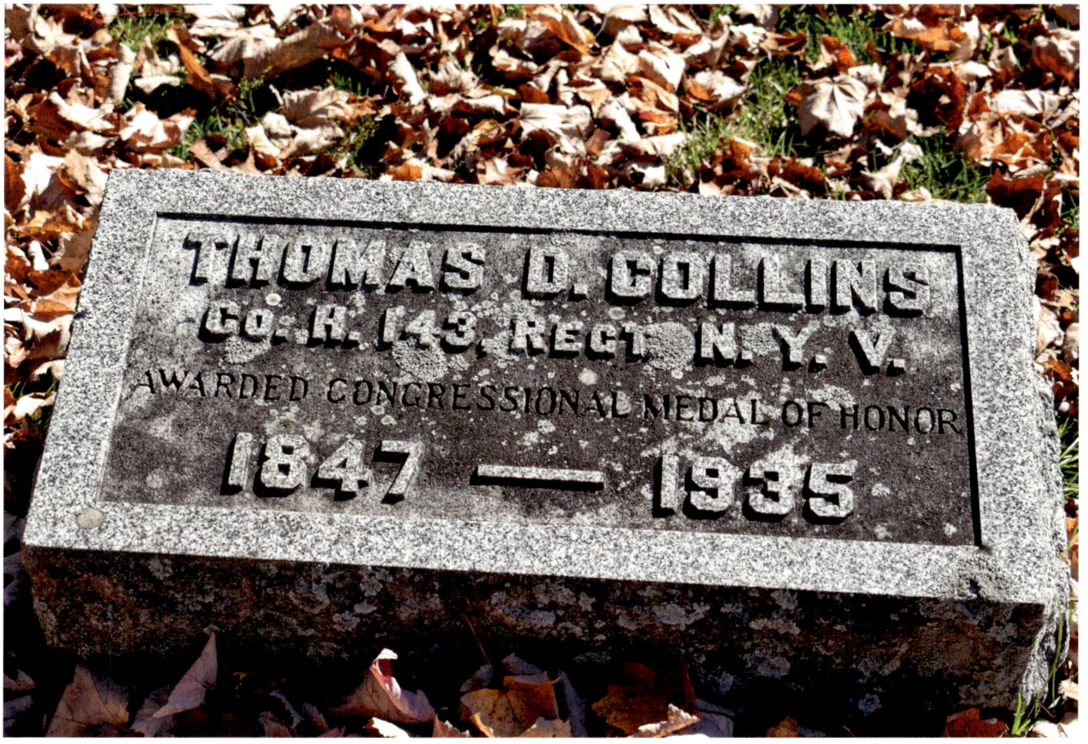

Thomas Collins was awarded the Medal of Honor for his courage on the battlefield.

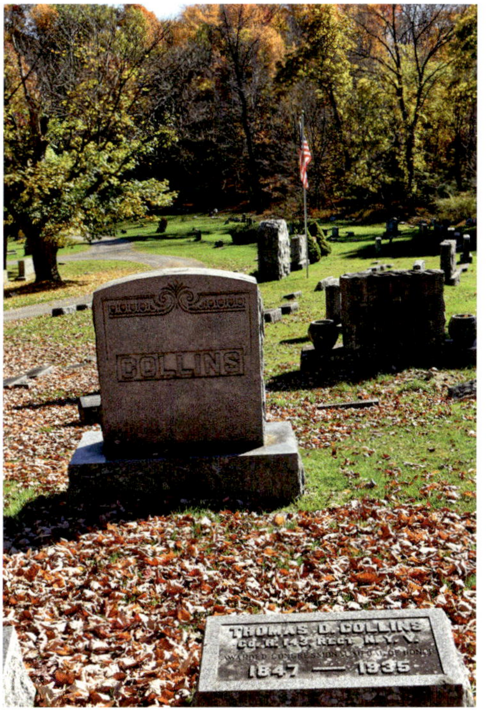

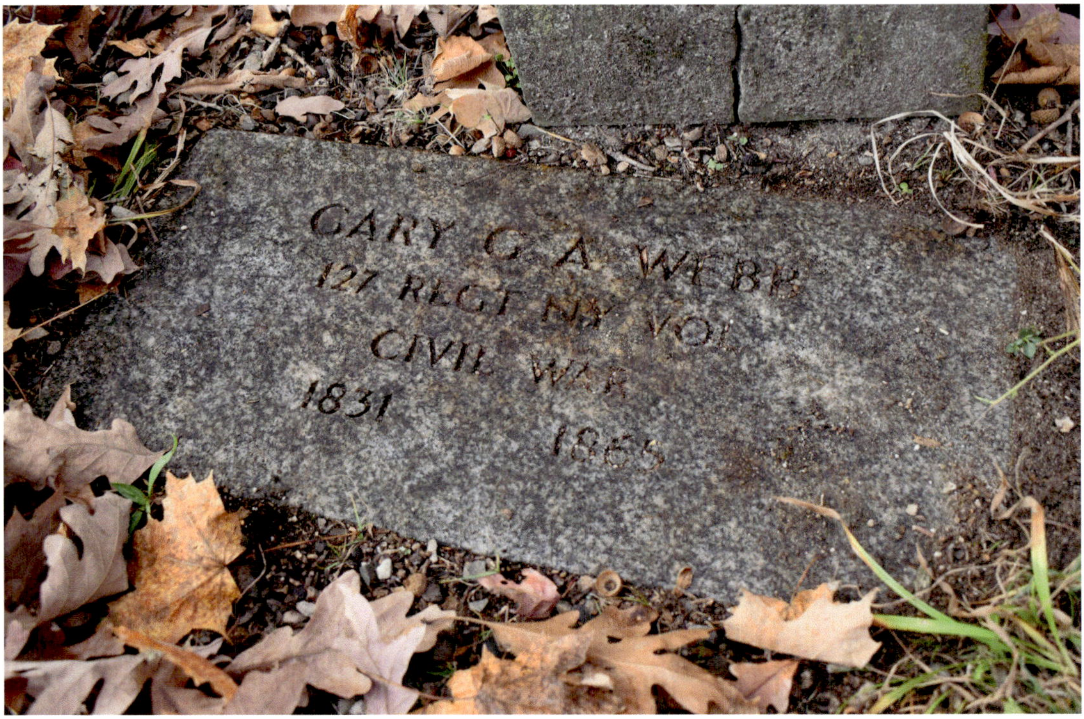

Gary Webb was killed while fighting during the war.

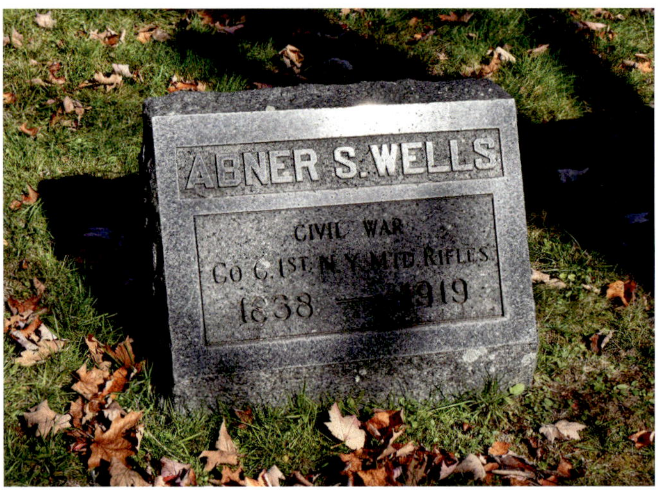

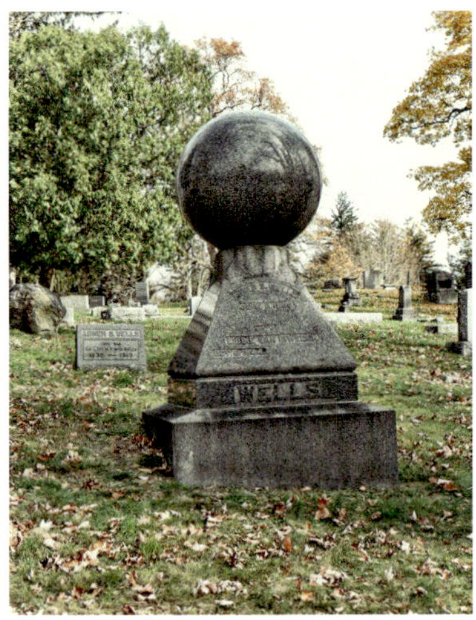

The spherical monument at the Abner Wells burial site is the only one of its kind in Hillside.

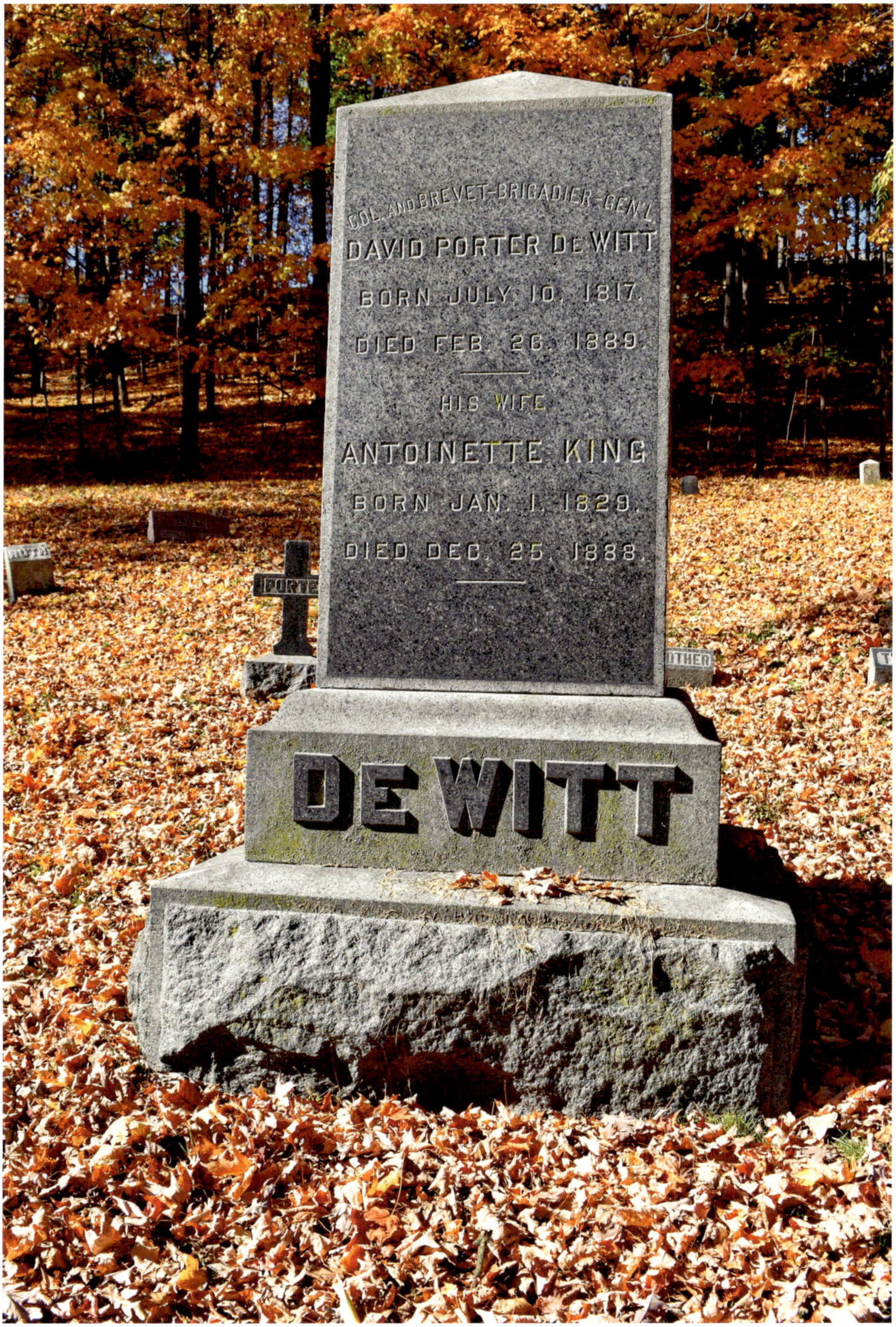

The graves of David Porter DeWitt and family are resting on a leafy incline that overlooks the pond.

4

Influential Families of Hillside

It's interesting to note that many of these families have traveled the world and some even lived in other places, yet they still chose Hillside to spend the rest of eternity. Philanthropists, socialites, millionaires, and prosperous politicians are buried here; many of them worked to create a better community while they were alive, while some continue to leave a legacy after death.

Thrall Family

S. Maretta Thrall (unknown–1897) was the widow of John W. Thrall, a wholesale grocer, and the daughter of Albert E. Babock and Margaret Laraway. While Mrs. Thrall was still living, she donated funds to help establish Thrall Hospital and Thrall Park. After her death, Mrs. Thrall donated $30,000 to the city to fund a public library. The Thrall Library was opened in 1901 on Orchard Street. Mrs. Thrall's family plot is with her husband and parents in Hillside.

Horton and Morrison Family

Webb Horton (1826–1908) at one time was considered one of the wealthiest men in the East. He came from the Pennsylvania oil fields and he ran a successful tannery with his brother, Charles. At the turn of the century, construction began on his glorious mansion on South Street in Middletown. Designed by prestigious architect Frank Lindsey, the forty-room mansion and adjoining property boasted ponds, tunnels, tennis courts, a ballroom, Tiffany stained-glass windows, and a greenhouse. Webb died never having spent a night in his new home, also leaving a wife, Elizabeth (1833–1917), a daughter, Carrie (1861–1910), and a son, Eugene (1856–1918). Another son, Junius Ray (1860–1879) died years earlier while attending military academy. Carrie was rumored to socialize with European royalty; allegedly she was in love with a Prussian count. Eugene loved a local woman who died from tuberculosis, and he remained a heartbroken bachelor his entire life.

After Eugene's passing from the flu in 1918, the family mansion was bequeathed to Eugene's cousin, John H. Morrison, Sr. (1881–1946), and his wife, Christine (1879–1977). The generous Mrs. Morrison was never comfortable living such a lavish life, and shortly after John's death, she donated the mansion to be utilized as a community college in 1950. In fact, it was New York's first county-endorsed college. Today, Morrison Hall is still in use as an administration building on the college campus.

In 1914, the Webb Horton Memorial Presbyterian Church was dedicated to the memory of Webb Horton by Elizabeth and Eugene. In 1918, after the reading of Eugene's will, money was donated to build the Elizabeth A. Horton Memorial Hospital in honor of his mother. The new hospital opened in 1929. The Horton family is buried together, as are the Morrisons.

Stivers Family

Moses D. Stivers (1828–1895) was a man of many skills. He married Mary Stewart (1834–1915), who came from a prominent family. Stivers farmed, taught school, ran a general store, and then a dry goods store. In 1868, he bought the *Orange County Press* and his interest in journalism remained strong until his death. He was a teacher, a bank president, county clerk, a tax collector, and a U.S. congressman from 1889–1891. Stivers was on many boards, including the state hospital and Hillside Cemetery. His son, John D. Stivers (1861–1935), followed in his father's footsteps, publishing the *Middletown Daily Times* with his brother, Lewis (1859–1905). In his lifetime, he was also postmaster, an assemblyman, and senator. John Stivers was found dead sitting at his desk in 1935. The Stivers family is buried together, including Lewis and Dr. Moses A. (1872–1960).

Hulse and Curtis Family

Captain Thomas E. Hulse (1796–1881) and his wife, Permelia, are buried in Hillside under a weathered angel with a broken wing. Capt. Hulse owned a number of schooners and steamboats on the Hudson River, including the popular *Thomas E. Hulse* vessel. One of his nine children, Harriet Augusta (1832–1919), married Sylvester J. Curtis (1826–1899). Curtis was one of the oldest members of the New York Stock Exchange, and he had made a fortune over his lifetime. Although Sylvester and Harriet considered Manhattan their home, they frequented Middletown to visit the Hulse homestead. After the passing of Mr. Curtis in 1899, Mrs. Curtis and her daughter, Harriet Louisa (1855–1919), moved to New Jersey to stay with her son, Thomas E. H. Curtis (1852–1915). After Thomas died in 1915, Mrs. Curtis and her daughter stayed in boarding houses and fancy hotels, including the Waldorf-Astoria. The ladies ultimately wound up in Middletown with family, as the elder Harriet was her daughter's caretaker. Sadly, Mrs. Curtis outlived her daughter by fifteen days, both women passing in January 1919. At the time of her death, Mrs. Curtis was a wealthy woman; in her will, she left a large portion of her estate to her lawyers and their relatives. Her granddaughters contested the will, claiming she was not of sound mind when she made her arrangements. Mrs. Curtis was an art collector, and one of her cherished paintings was *Moonlight* by famed artist Ralph Albert Blakelock. Incidentally, Blakelock was a longtime resident of the Middletown State Hospital. Across the cemetery from the Hulse angel, the elaborate Curtis monument is immense; the figure on the top has an anchor at her feet, and she is pointing to the heavens.

Low Family

Henry Reynolds Low (1826–1888) was born in Fallsburg, New York, in Sullivan County. He began his career as a teacher and a farmer. He opened Monticello Academy with his brother, Benjamin, in 1849. He practiced law and was a county judge prior to coming to Middletown in 1867. Upon his arrival, he opened a law office and invested in the railroad and real estate. Low was a state senator from 1861–1866, and again in 1883–1888. In 1884, he was chairman of the Senate Oleomargarine Investigating Committee and was the originator of the Oleomargarine Bill. In 1888, the year of his death, he introduced a bill to incorporate Middletown as a city, and by that following summer, Middletown's status changed from village to city.

Also, it is interesting to note that Low's grandfather and namesake was a Quaker named Henry Reynolds. He was politically outspoken, and several attempts were made to kill Henry by a vengeful Tory gang during the Revolution. One night in 1782, Henry's twelve-year-old daughter, Phebe, Henry Low's future aunt, fought back against those attacks. She saved her father from certain death in his own house, by cutting him down out of his noose twice and tending to his stab wounds. The family survived fires and beatings, and in 1788, they moved to the Neversink area of Sullivan County, New York, where Reynolds was the first town supervisor and an assemblyman. Both Henry and Phebe are interred in Neversink.

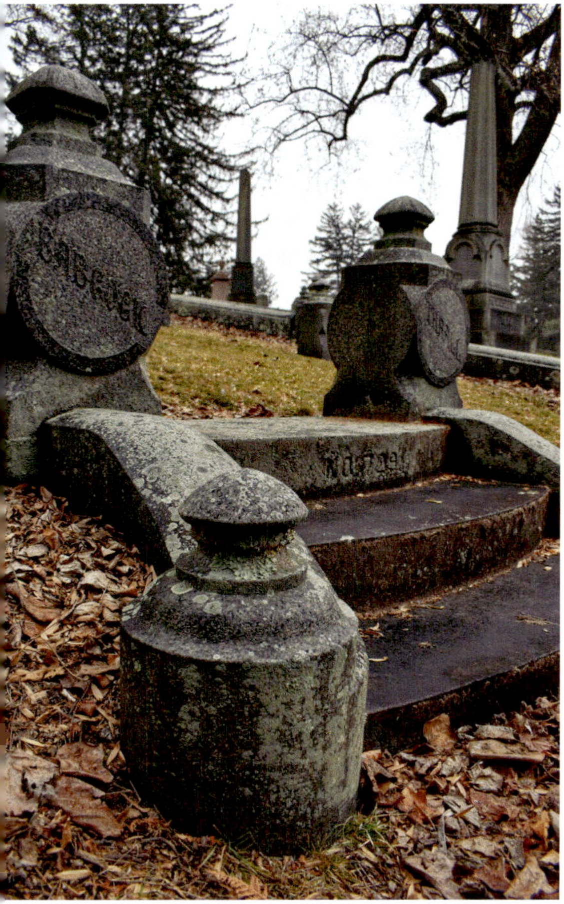

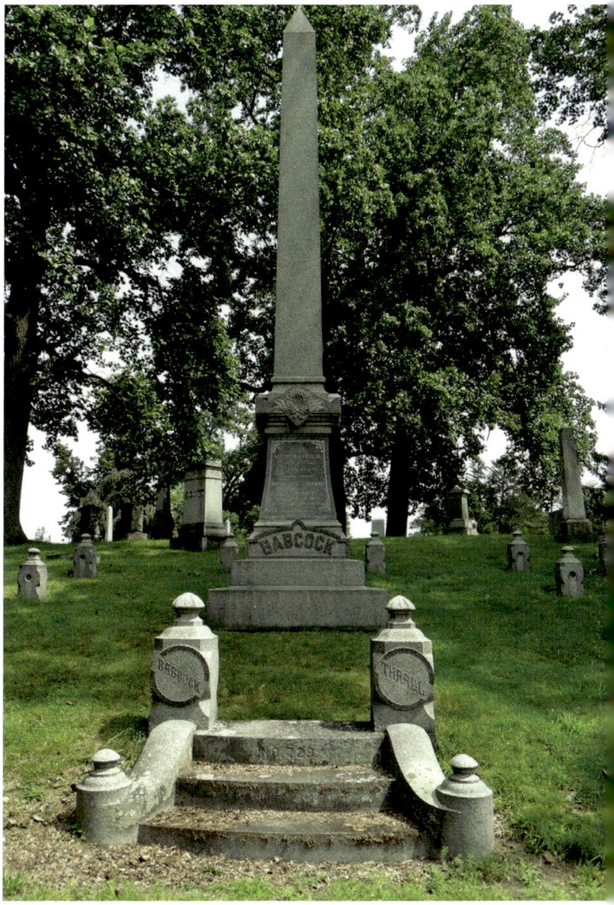

Judging by the posts surrounding the Thrall/Babcock plot, ironwork was either stolen or intentionally removed to deter theft years ago.

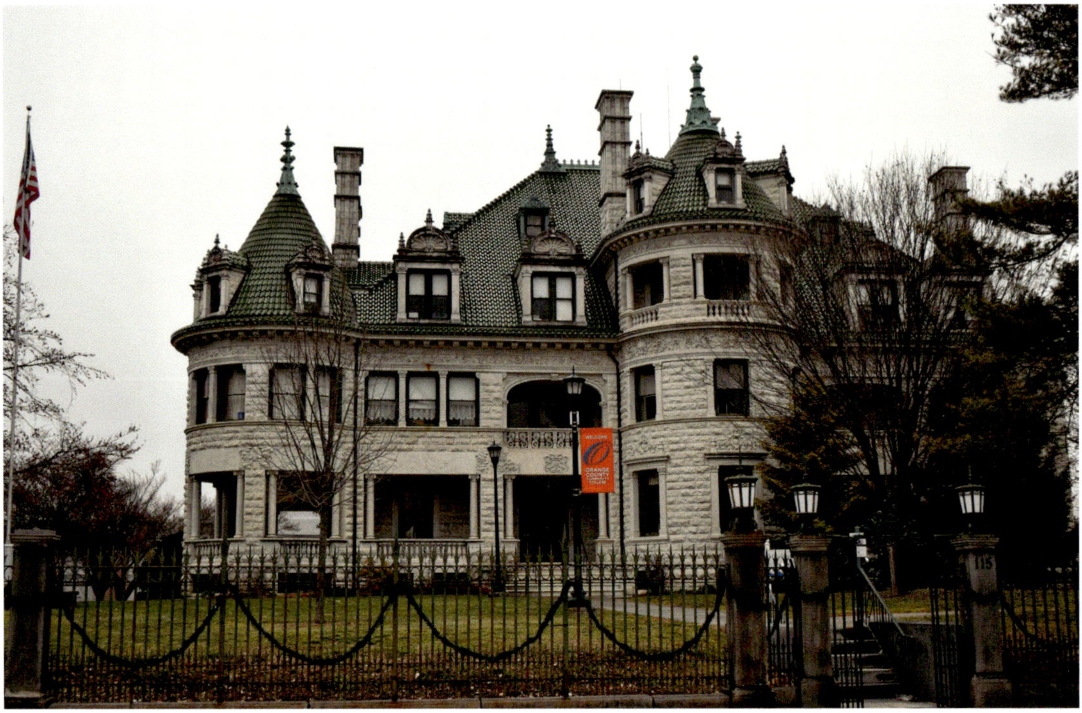

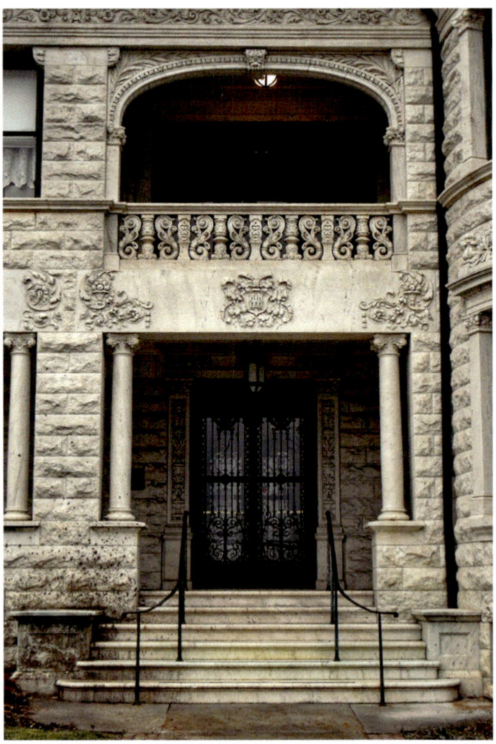

Above: Webb Horton's mansion, also known as Morrison Hall, as seen from the street.

Left: The front entrance of the Horton mansion is quite impressive.

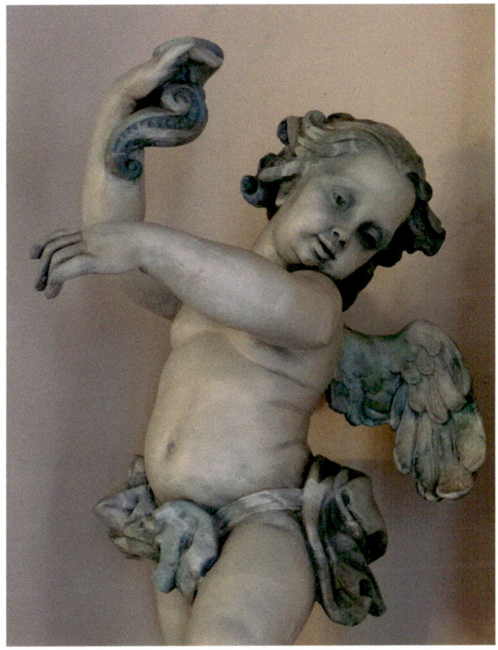

Right: In one of the interior rooms in the mansion, a whimsical cherub strikes a pose.

Below: An exquisite stained-glass window was installed inside the Horton mansion.

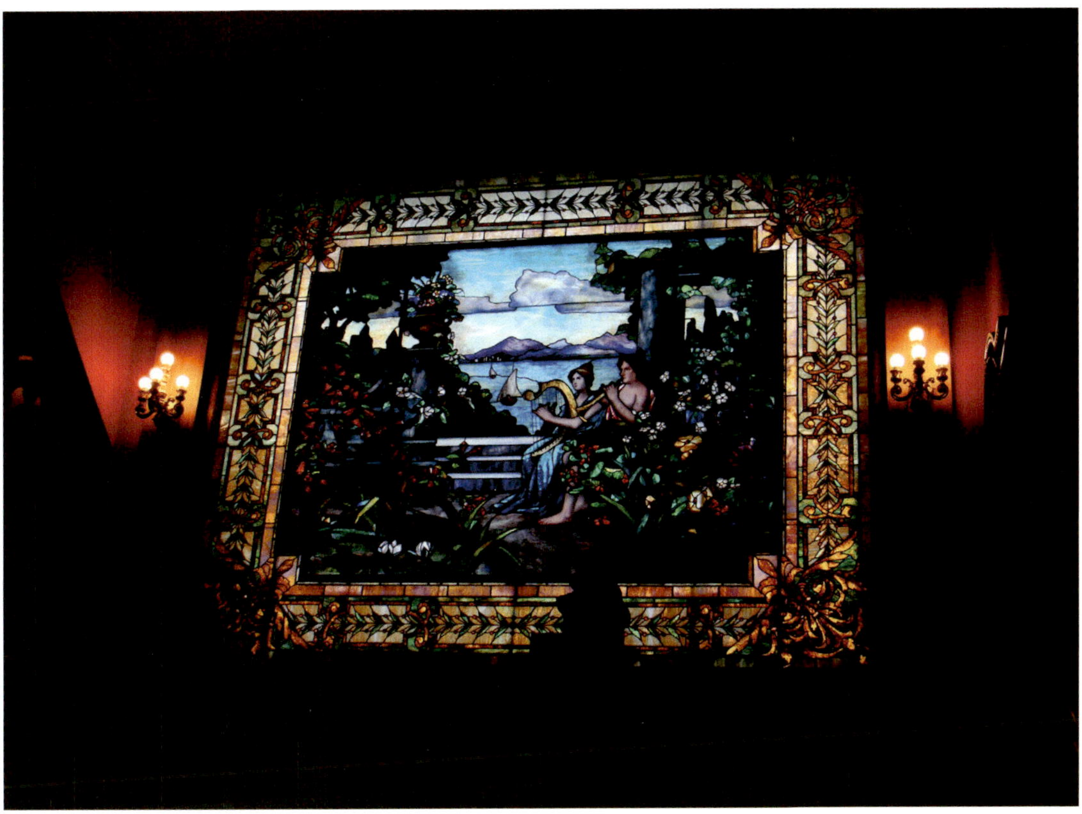

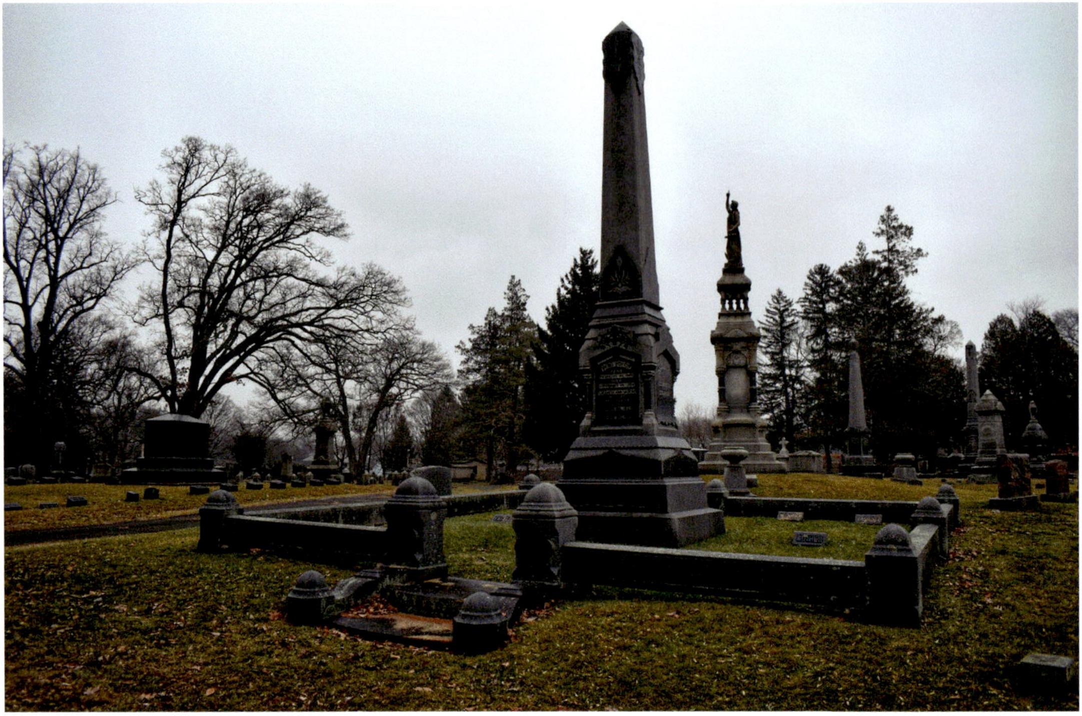

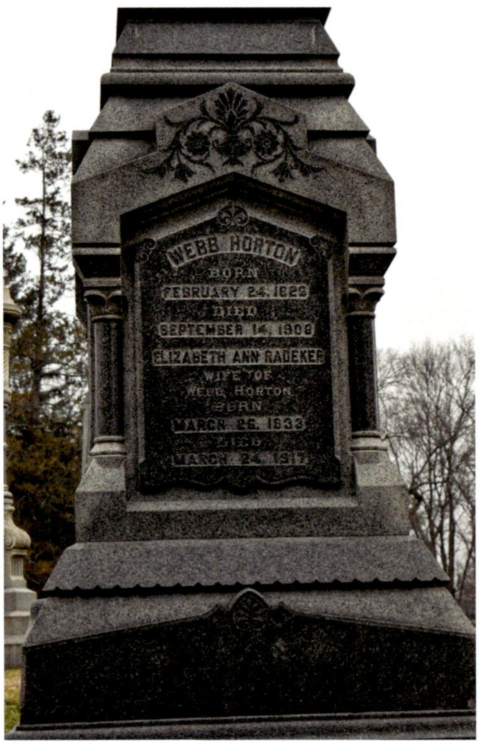

Above, left and opposite: Webb Horton's decorated obelisk can easily be seen from many points in the cemetery.

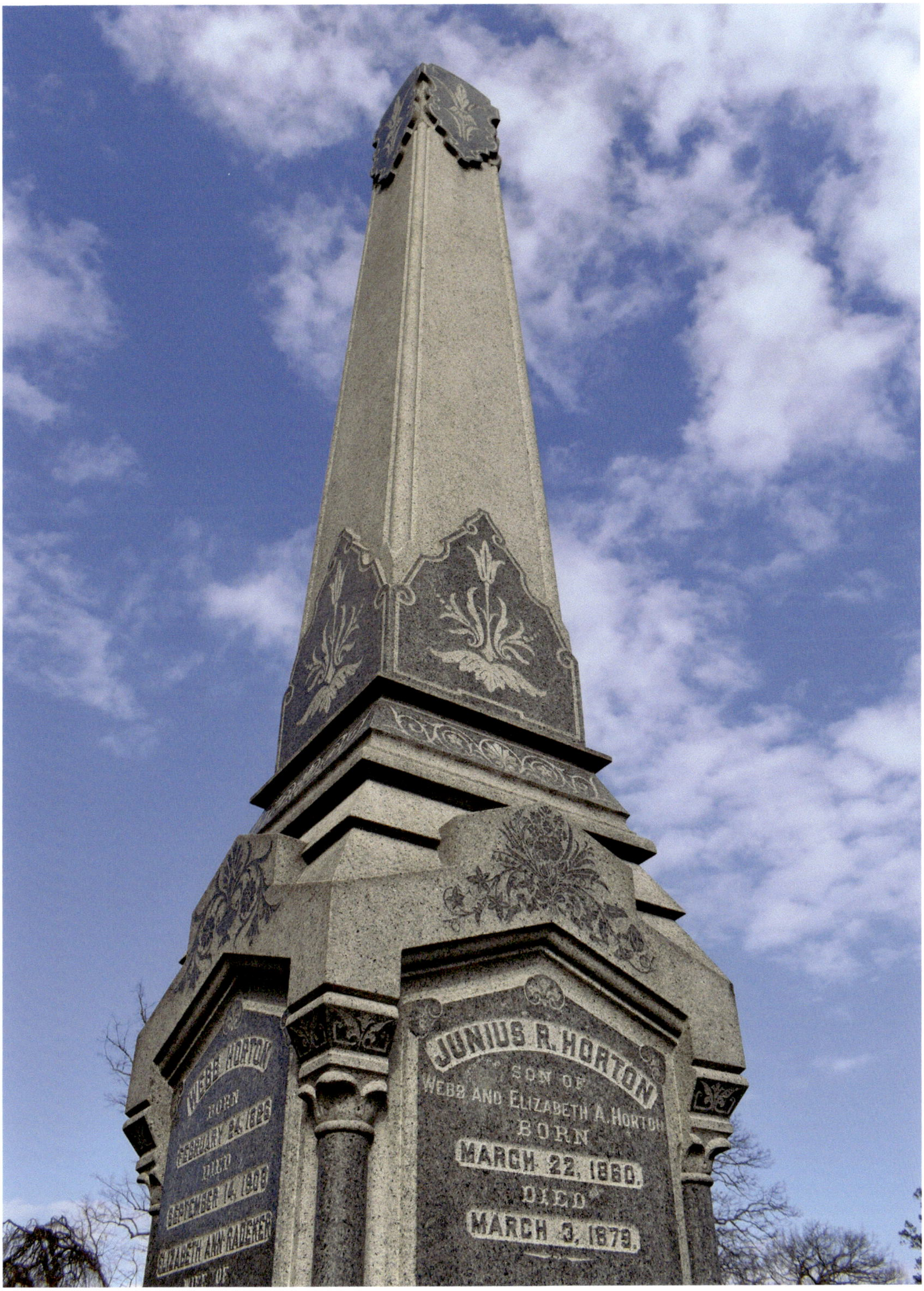
WEBB HORTON
BORN
FEBRUARY 24, 1826
DIED
SEPTEMBER 14, 1908
ELIZABETH ANN RADEKER
JUNIUS R. HORTON
SON OF
WEBB AND ELIZABETH A. HORTON
BORN
MARCH 22, 1860.
DIED
MARCH 3, 1879.

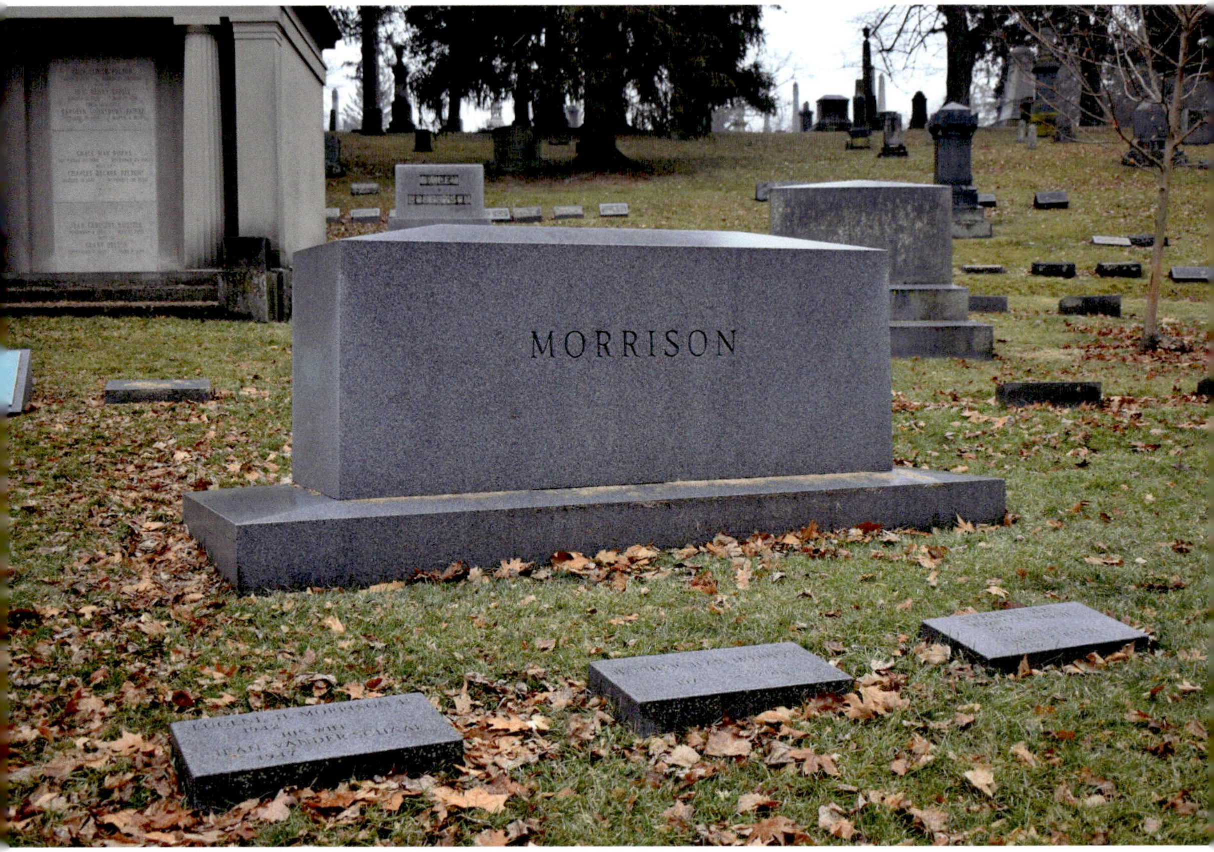

John and Christine Morrison are laid to rest in the Morrison plot.

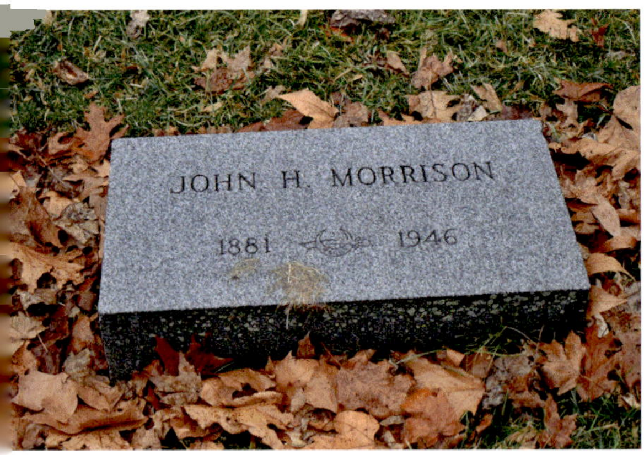

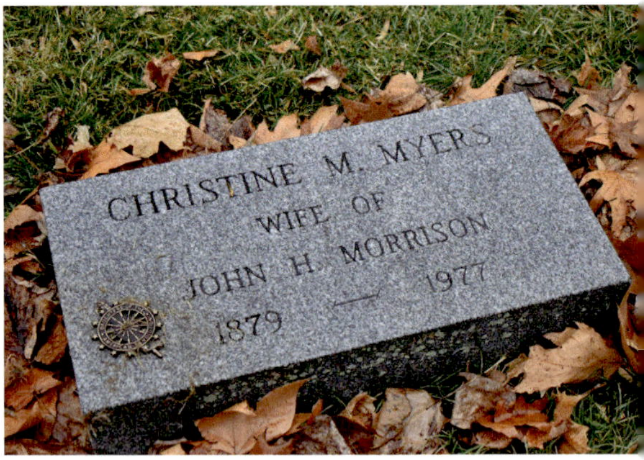

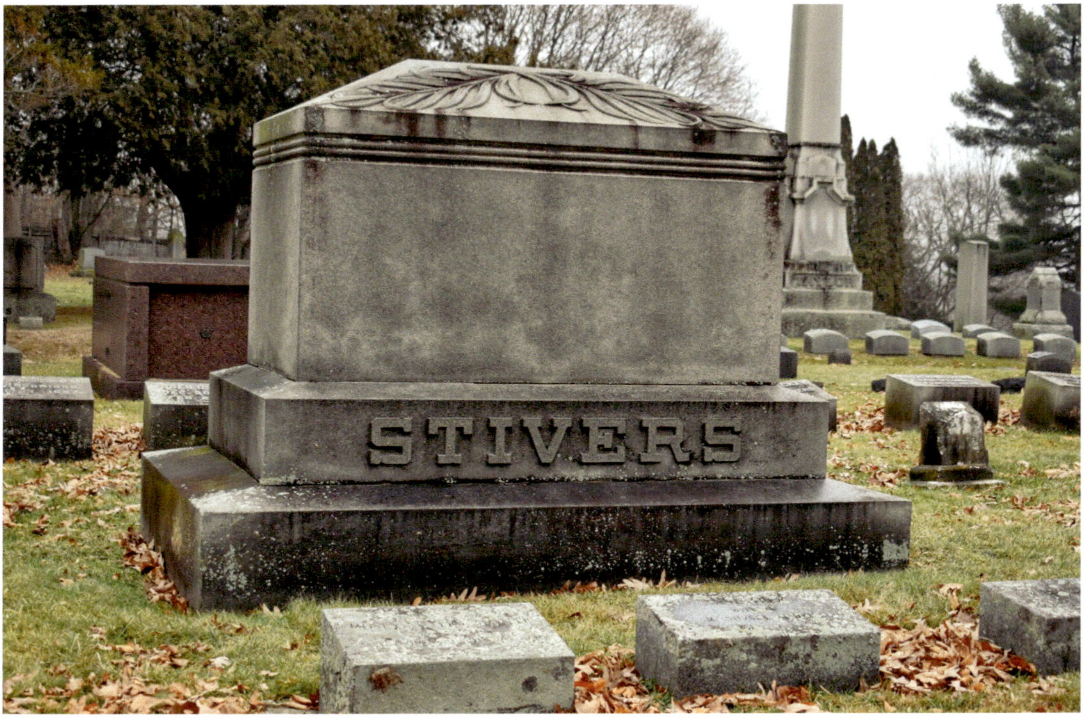

The Stivers family, including Moses D., are interred together.

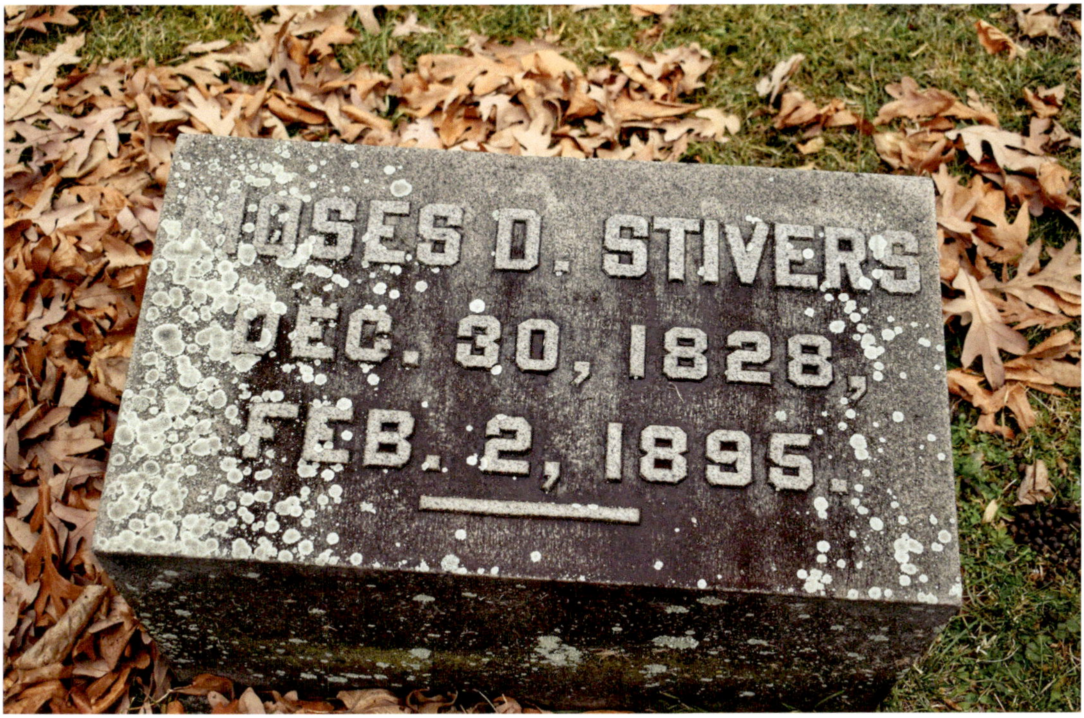

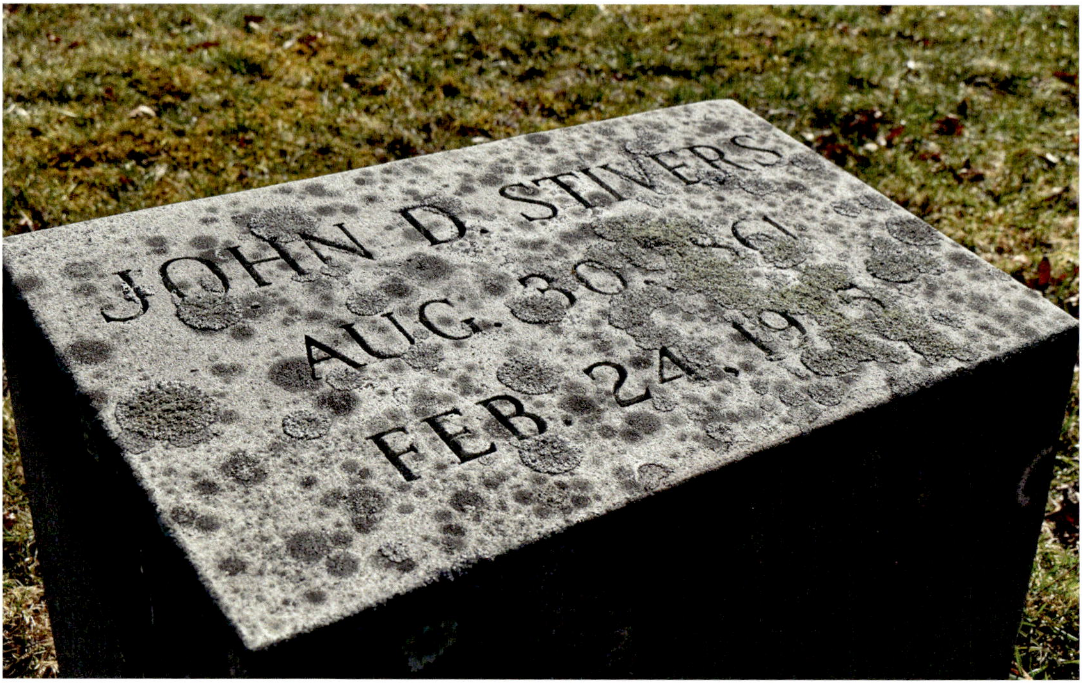
JOHN D. STIVERS
AUG. 30
FEB. 24

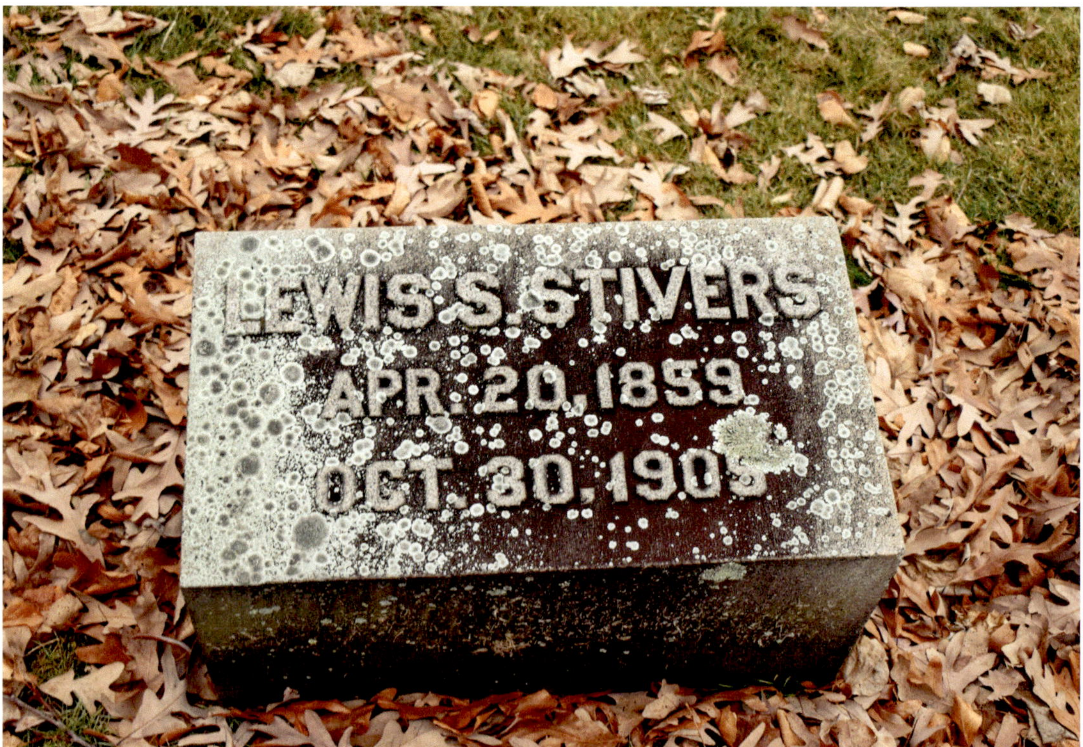
LEWIS S. STIVERS
APR. 20, 1859
OCT. 30, 190

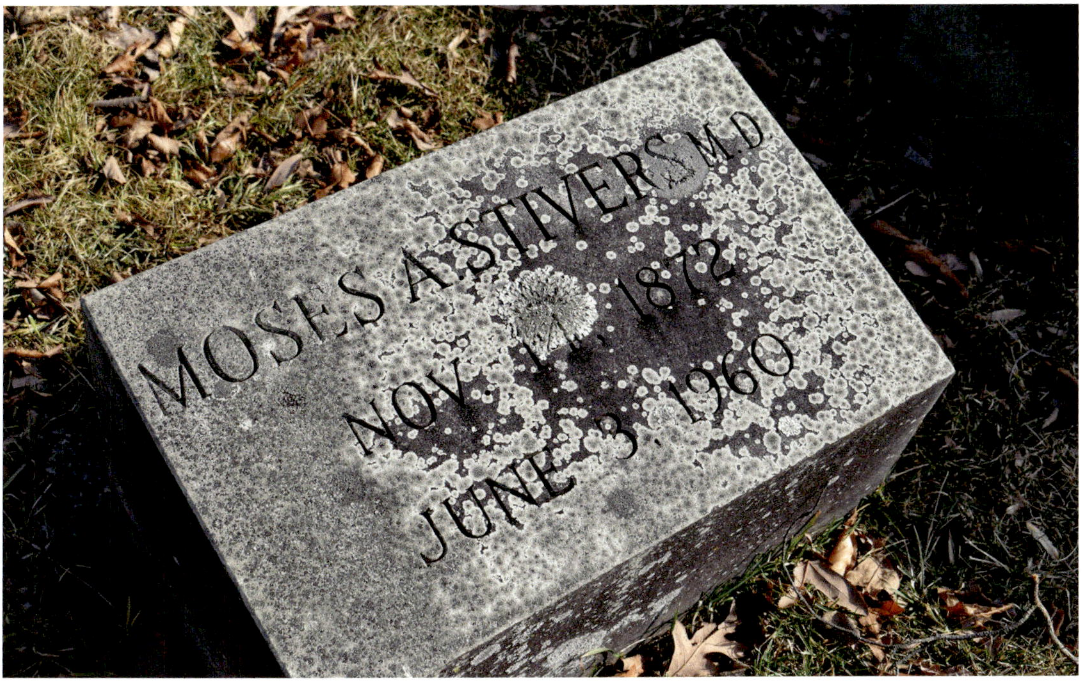

Above and opposite page: John, Lewis, and Moses A. Stivers are buried next to their father, Moses D.

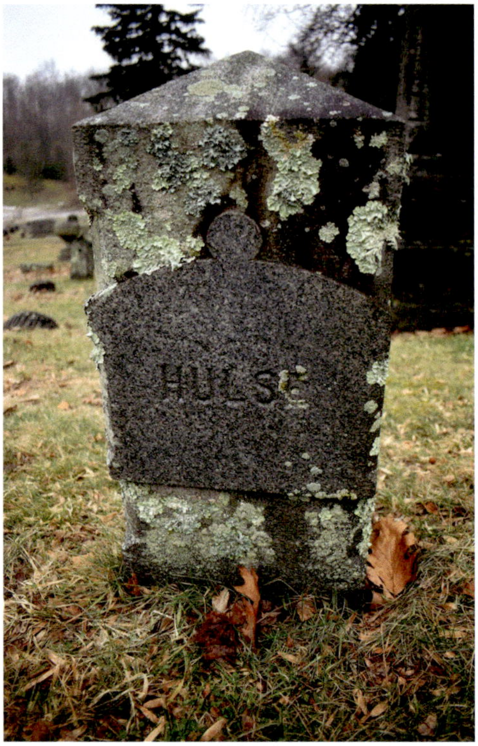

Left: This weathered post marks the corner of the Thomas E. Hulse plot.

Below left: The epitaphs for Thomas and his wife, Permelia, are engraved on the base of the Hulse angel.

Below right: Hulse's angel stands solemnly on a summer day.

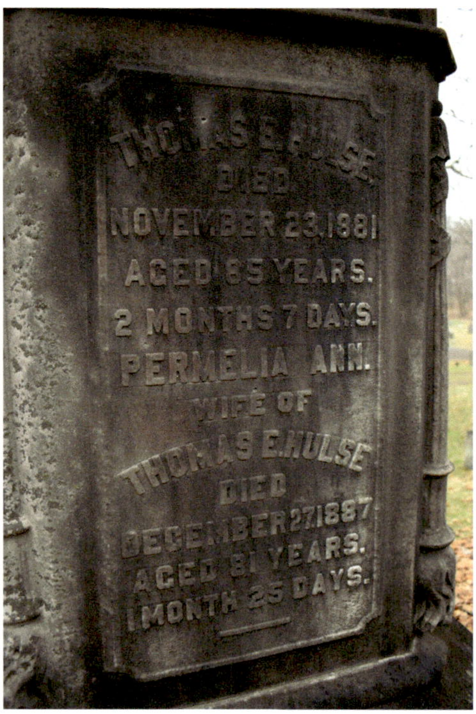

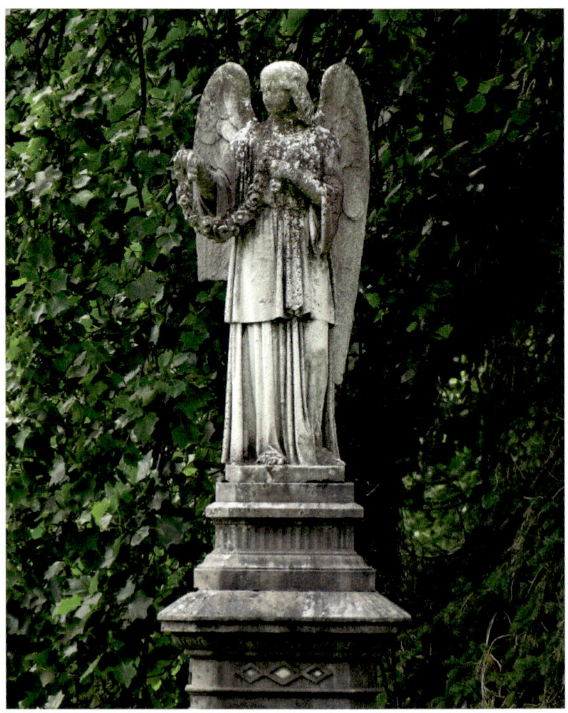

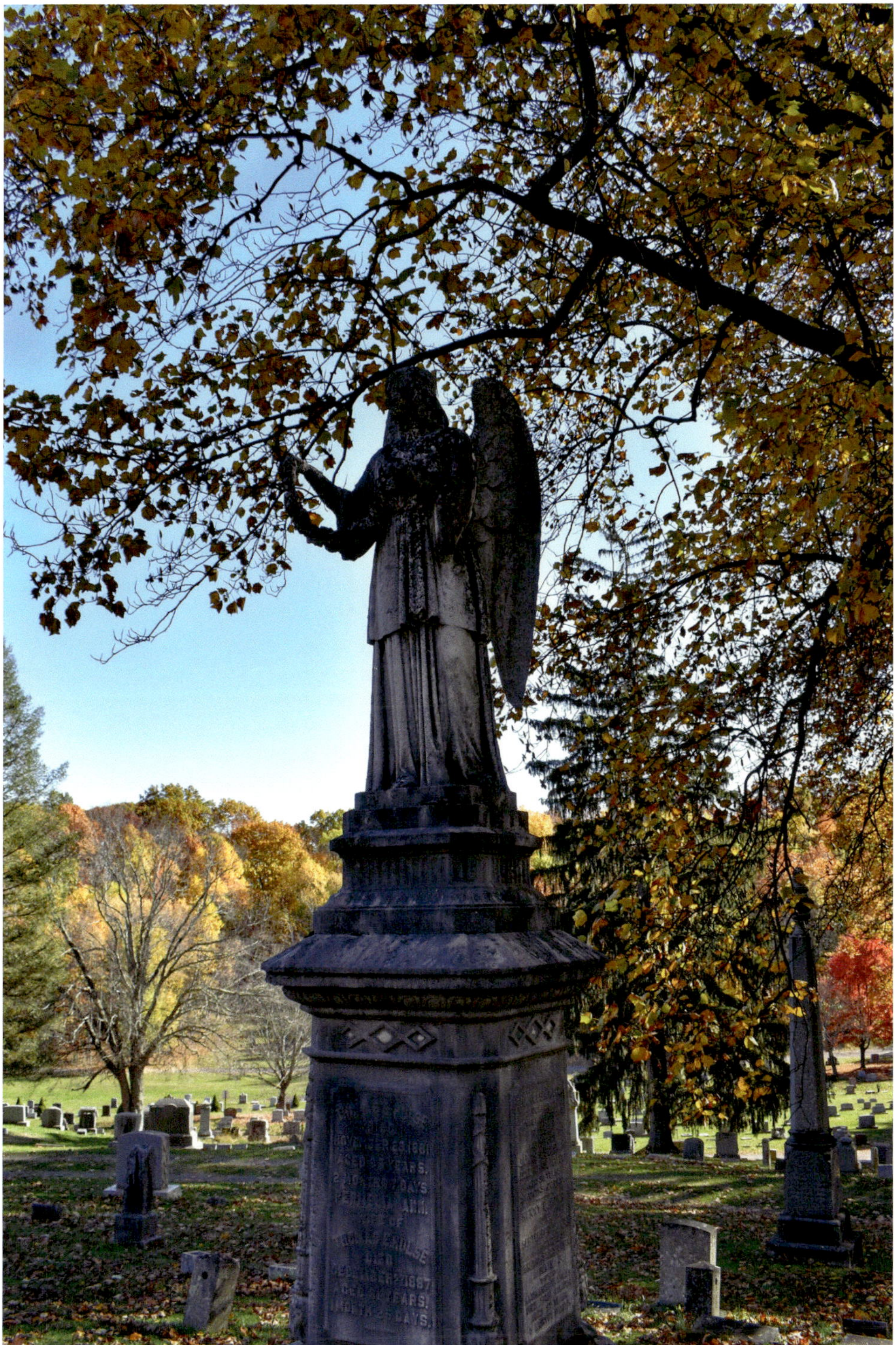

The Hulse angel is perched on a quiet knoll surrounded by blazing colors of autumn.

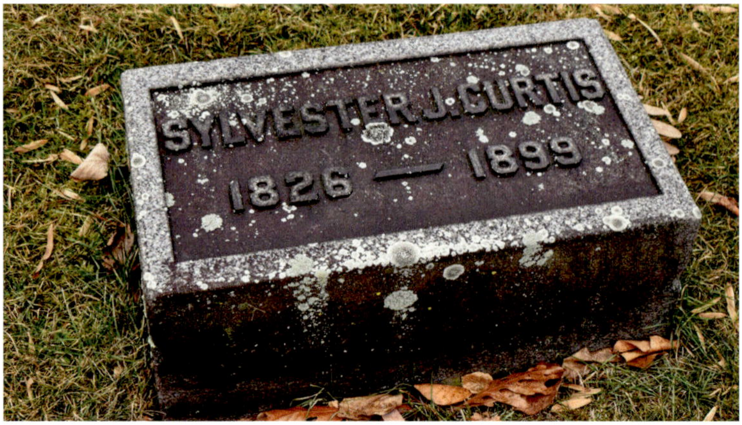

Under the massive Curtis monument lie the bodies of Sylvester, Harriet L., and Mrs. Harriet A. Curtis.

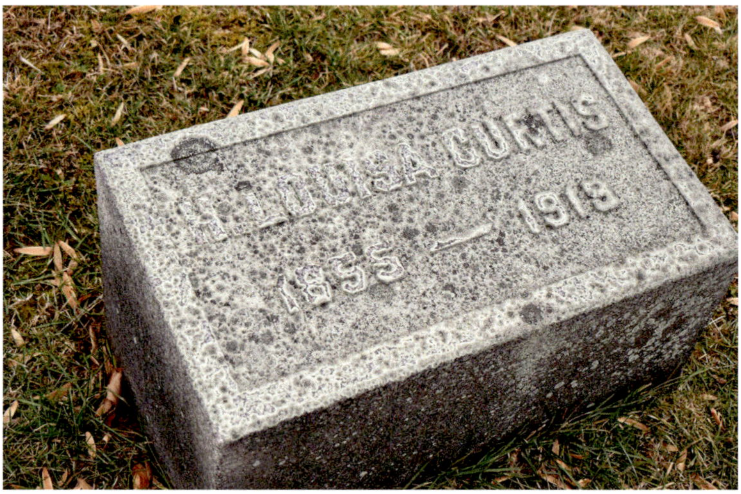

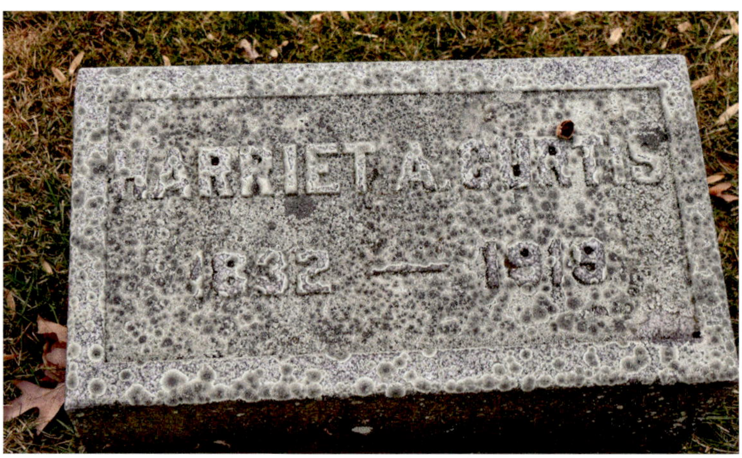

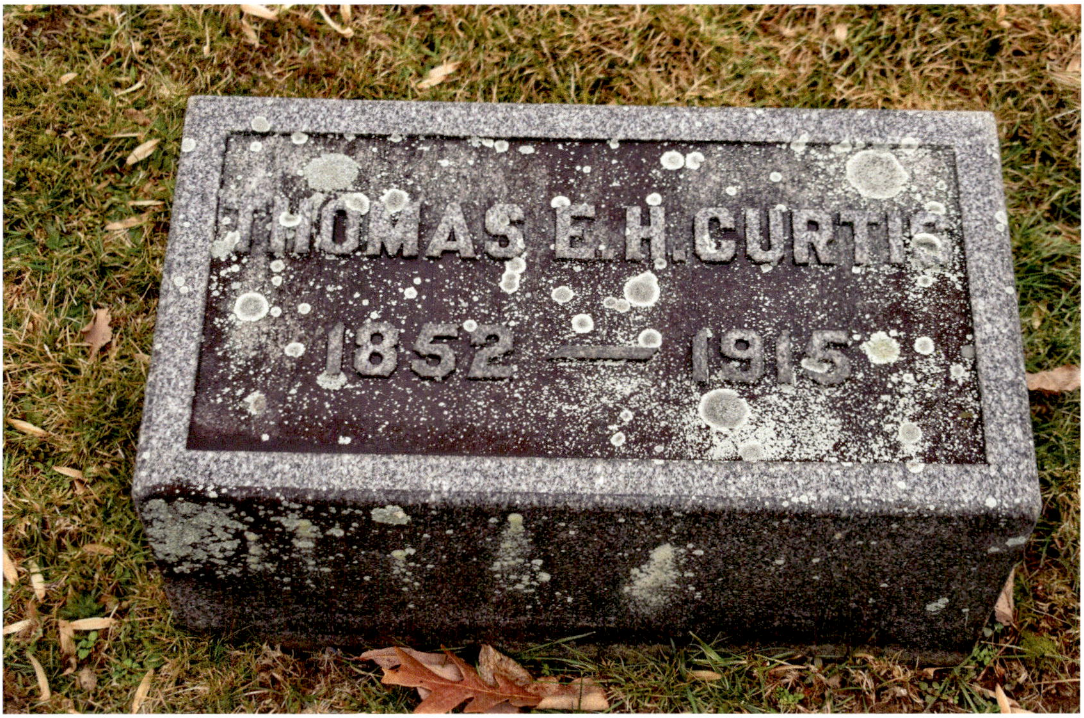

Above: The son of Sylvester and Harriet, Thomas E. H. Curtis was a friend of President Woodrow Wilson. According to his obituary in the *Middletown Times Press*, he was a "man of brilliant mind and high moral character."

Right: The Curtis memorial appears to reach to the heavens as it diminishes many of the tall obelisks around it.

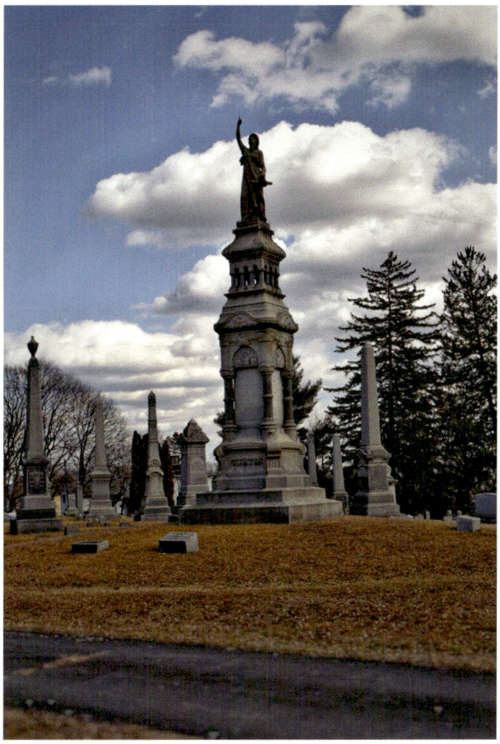

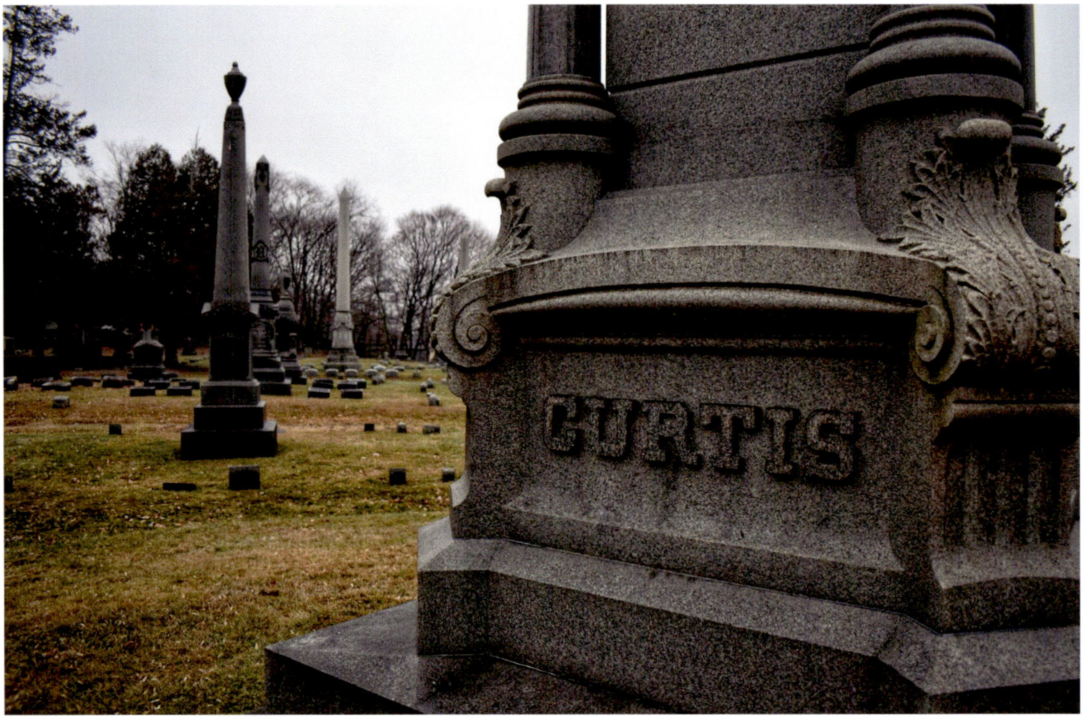

Not only is the Curtis monument towering, but it has quite beautiful details in its design.

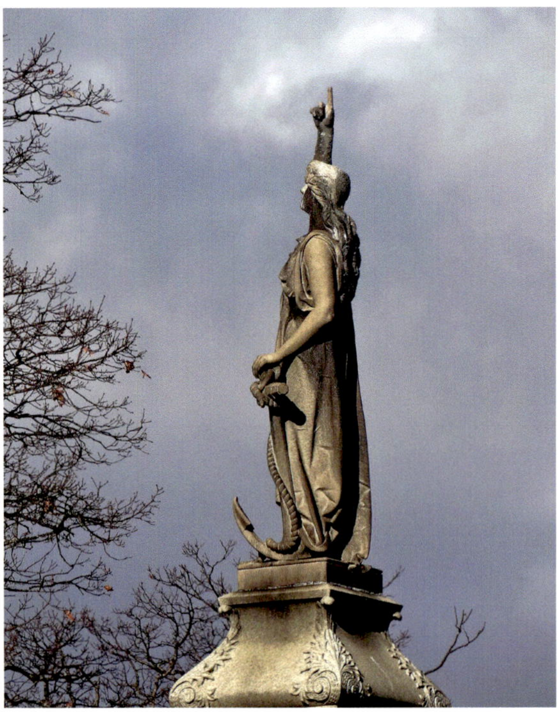

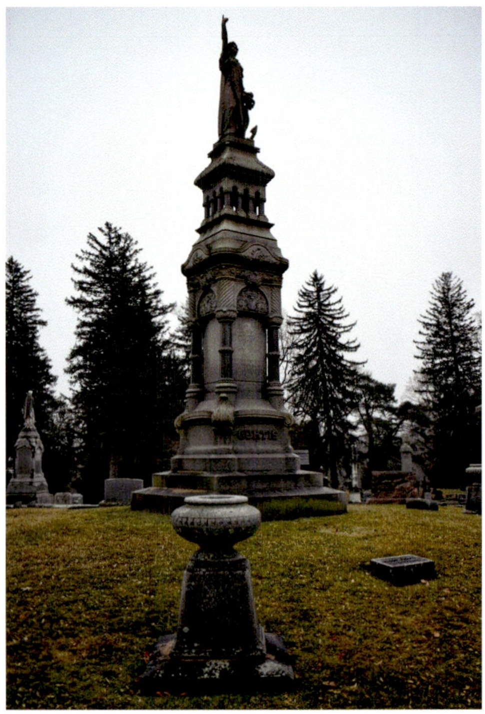

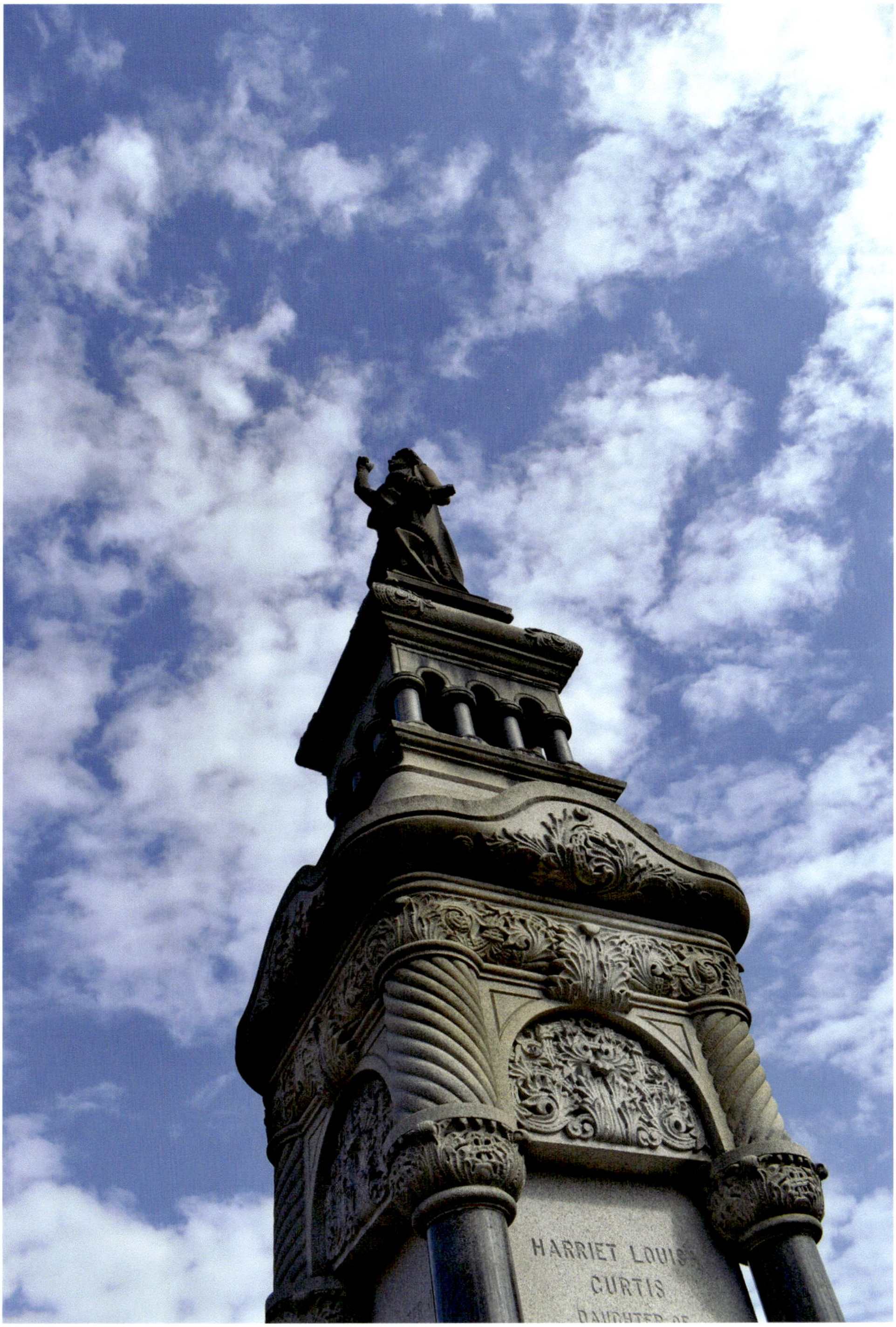

The wispy clouds and brilliant blue sky enhance the incredible elegance of the Curtis memorial.

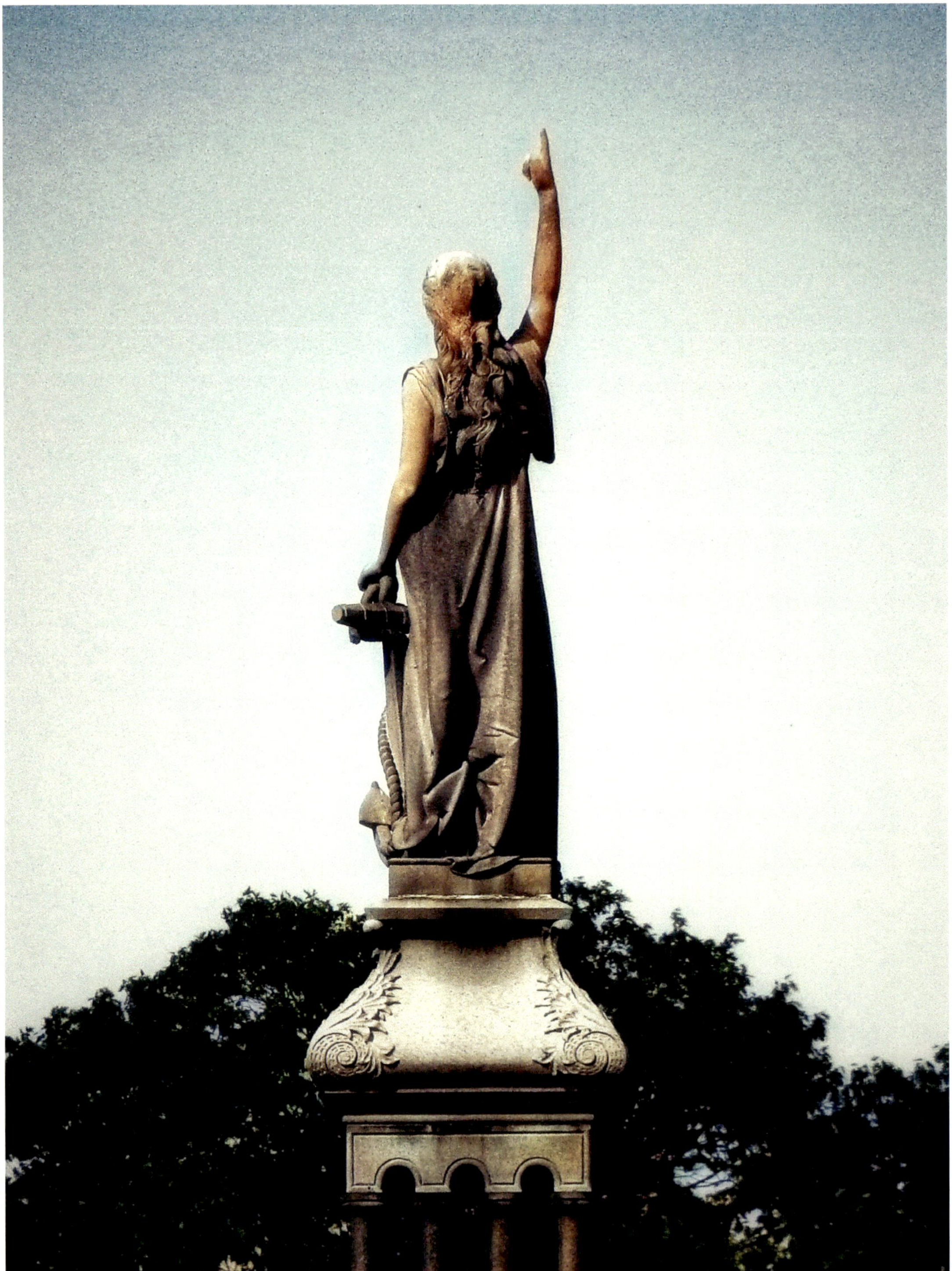

An anchor symbolizes hope in funerary art, as seen here on the Curtis statue.

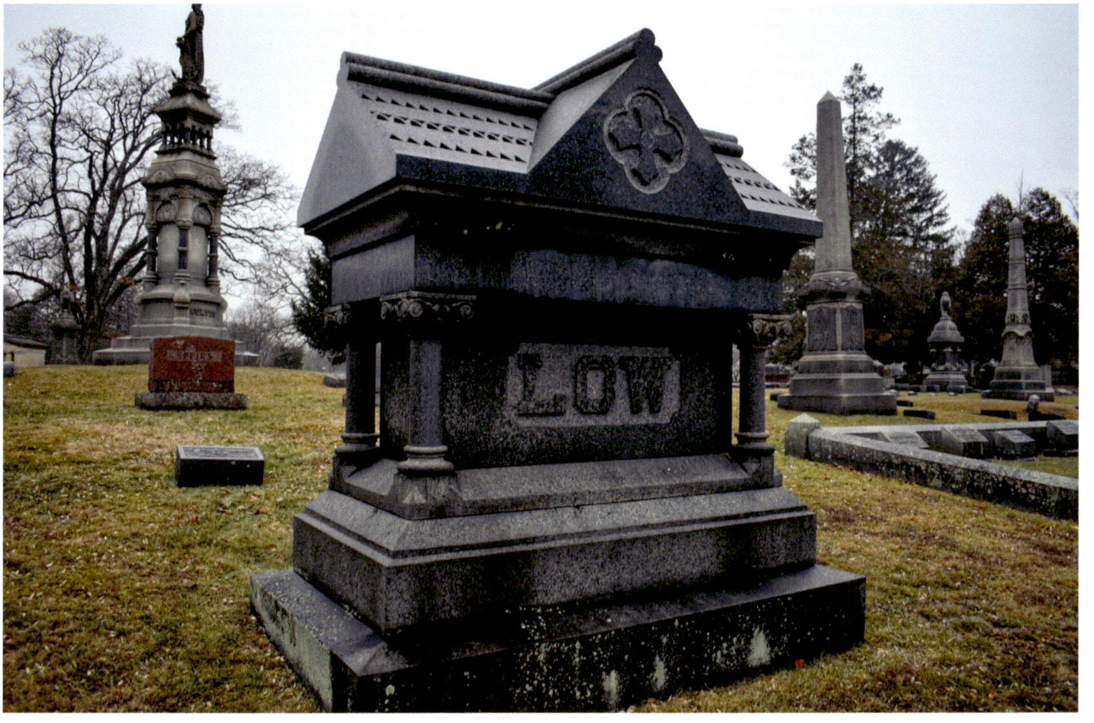

Henry Reynolds Low has a unique house-shaped monument at his burial site.

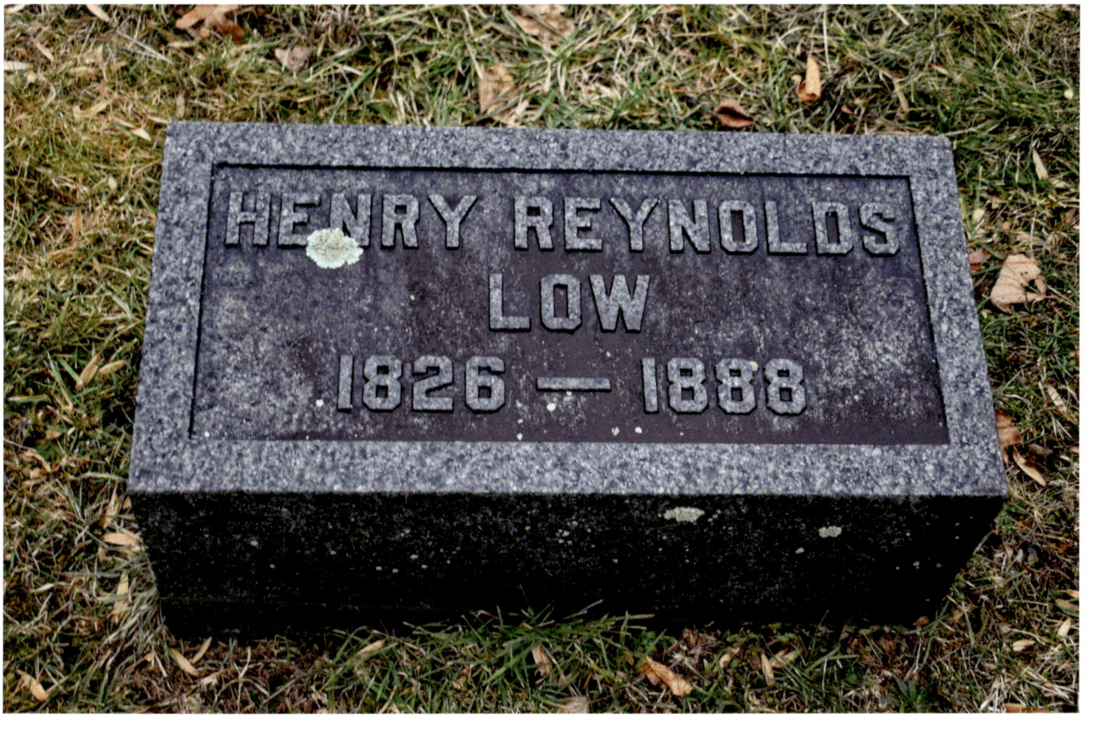

5

Industry Pioneers & Businessmen of Hillside

The backbone of any community are the laborers, the inventors, and the visionaries. Many pivotal entrepreneurs have chosen Hillside as their final resting place with their families, and their achievements still impact our world today.

John Augustine Hartford (1872–1951) and his wife, Pauline, who were married twice, are buried in the Corwin plot in Hillside. In 1888, Mr. Hartford joined the Atlantic & Pacific Tea Company to work alongside his brother, George Jr., and his father. As the company grew under the leadership of the Hartfords, so did the opportunities for John Hartford. He served as president for "A & P" for thirty-five years until his death. During that time, product lines expanded, the number of stores grew, and ultimately, the first grocery store chain had been created. In fact, the modern supermarket as we know it today probably owes its existence to the Hartfords.

The John A. Hartford Foundation was established by John in 1929. It focused on healthcare, more recently for older Americans. In 1950, John and George Jr. were on the cover of *Time* magazine. In 1951, John died while attending a meeting in the Chrysler building. The Hartford's incredible summer mansion in Valhalla, New York, is currently part of Westchester Community College.

Elisha Pearl Wheeler (1807–1876) learned the stove and tin business at a young age. He arrived in Middletown just as the Erie Railroad did in 1843, and with E. M. Madden, a former apprentice of Wheeler's, formed the Orange County Furnace Company. The foundry was the first important industry in Middletown. Wheeler was involved in other businesses with Madden, including the Eagle File Company and the Monhagen Saw Works. In 1853, the saw factory was started as one of the first in the country, and by the 1870s, it was one of the largest. Wheeler was heavily involved in promoting prosperity and growth, serving as director for many organizations and committees. Railroads, plank roads, public forums, and banks existed because of Wheeler's dedication. Due to the failure of one of the railroads and other economic factors, it was said that Wheeler died penniless, although his obituary clearly states his widow would be quite comfortable in the years to follow.

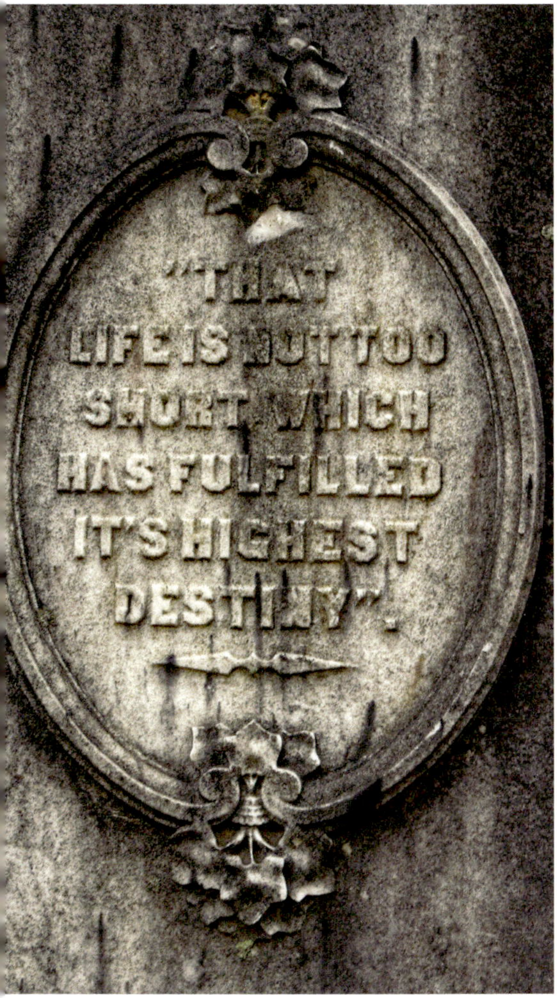

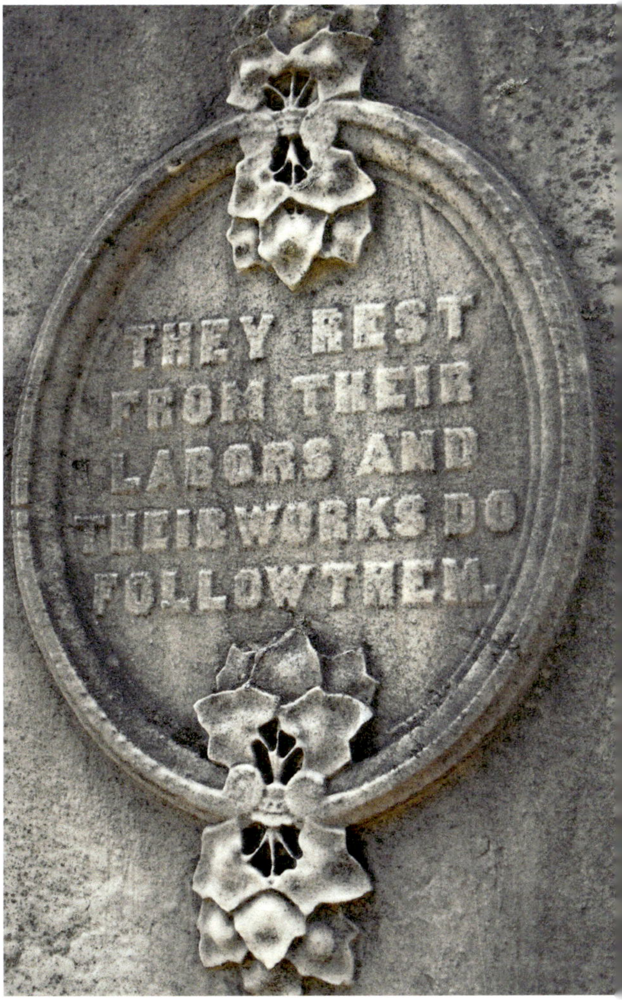

Above left: An inspiring inscription is carved on the grave of Charles C. McQuoid (died 1866, aged thirty-five years).

Above right: Words of encouragement are engraved on the H. E. Horton (1804–1869) monument.

Edward Millspaugh Madden (1818–1885) was a runaway at nine and a tinsmith's apprentice by the time he was fifteen. With a few dollars in his pocket, Madden came to Middletown in 1839 and bought a tin shop. In the early 1840s, he formed Middletown's first major industry, the Orange County Furnace Company, along with E. P. Wheeler. Other business ventures include the Eagle File Company and the Monhagen Saw Works. Madden was a senator 1856–1857, 1872–1875, and 1880–1881. He sat on many local boards, promoted railroads, and rallied to improve many of the area's institutions. Madden's accomplishments and contributions are too numerous to list; he was essential to Middletown's expansion and economic success.

William Clemson (1821–1890) came from a long line of metalworkers. His ancestors as far back as the fifteenth century created armor suits for knights. Clemson was born in England, and at age twenty-one, he sailed to America, specifically to Boston, and spent a few years working for a saw manufacturer. His innovative ideas and inventions improved product quality and the manufacturing process. Others in the industry were impressed and he came to Middletown to work for the Monhagen Saw Works. Eventually, proving his ingenuity and business sense, he joined the firm, and Wheeler, Madden and Clemson was established in 1860. After the deaths of Wheeler and Madden, Clemson became the sole owner. Following the family legacy, son George Nathan (1854–1930) invented the set-tooth hacksaw blade and formed a business partnership with his brother, Richard W.: The Clemson Brothers. The company was known worldwide for their Star hacksaw blades. The lucrative company stayed in the Clemson family, even adding lawnmowers to their inventory. Today, the original factory houses a brewery; in fact, the new owner kept the original name to honor the history of the factory. The George N. Clemson family plot in Hillside includes members of the Schrade (known for their knives) and Cross families.

J.M. Matthews (1810–1874) with H. H. Hunt, had a factory that manufactured carpet bags. The building was the first to be lit by gas in 1859, and it was another one of the town's leading industries.

James Madison Horton (1835–1914) began working on his brother Timothy's farm as a young man. They started a family milk distributing business, which led to Horton buying an ice cream company in the 1860s. Horton's Ice Cream Company became the largest manufacturer and distributor in the world, achieving enormous success. Two decades after his death, the company changed hands and became known as Borden's. Despite the name change, Horton's recipes were still used right up through the 1960s. Horton's estate was worth almost three million dollars at the time of his passing. His wife, Mary Ann, predeceased him in 1876 and for nearly forty years, Horton would make the trip from his home in New York City to visit Mary's grave on the anniversary of her death.

Samuel Denton (1794–1885) arrived in Middletown in 1821. He purchased the Beakes store at Franklin Square in the center of town and operated a general store there until 1856. This property became known as "Denton's Corner." Running a store in those days was not an easy task; Denton would travel over twenty miles to Newburgh to catch a boat to New York City. He would buy enough goods to last at least six months, and then haul it back by wagon.

Albert Bull (1829–1900) built Middletown's first theater, Bull's Opera House. After the opening in 1871, P. T. Barnum and Edwin Booth were some of the famous acts who provided entertainment at the theater. Bull was prominent in other local organizations also, having been president of a bank and power company. He was a descendant of Sarah Wells, an orphan who, in 1712, became the first European to settle in nearby Goshen, New York.

Halstead Sweet (1806–1886) was the owner of Sweet's Hotel. Formerly known as the Railroad House, Sweet's Hotel attracted many famous patrons and travelers, which Sweet himself became acquainted with. He dabbled in politics; he was a town supervisor and the village president. Sweet enjoyed engaging in lively political discussions with his fellow Middletowners.

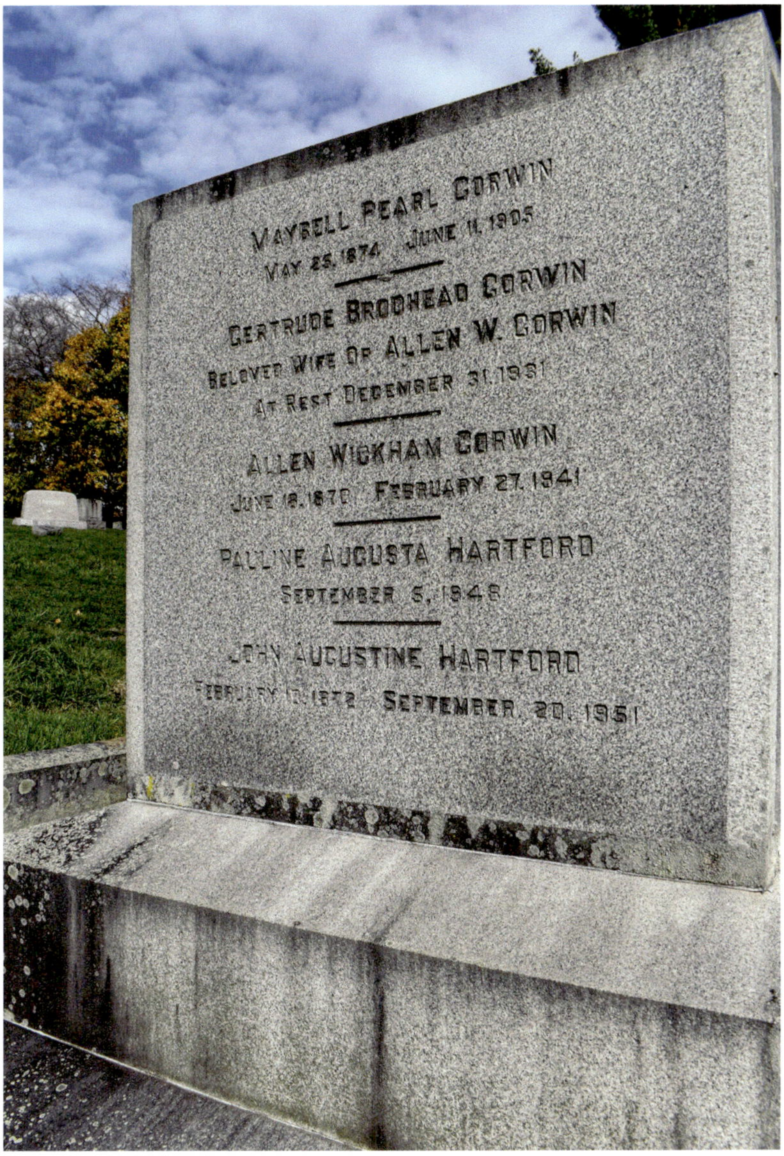

The epitaphs of John and Pauline Hartford are shown on the side of the enormous Corwin memorial.

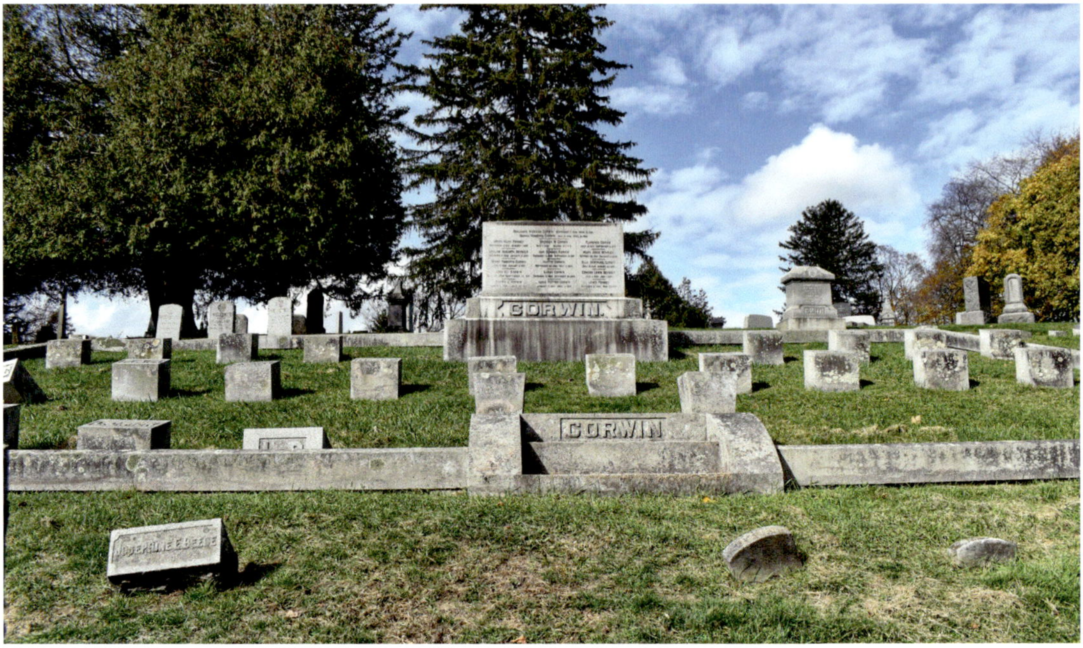

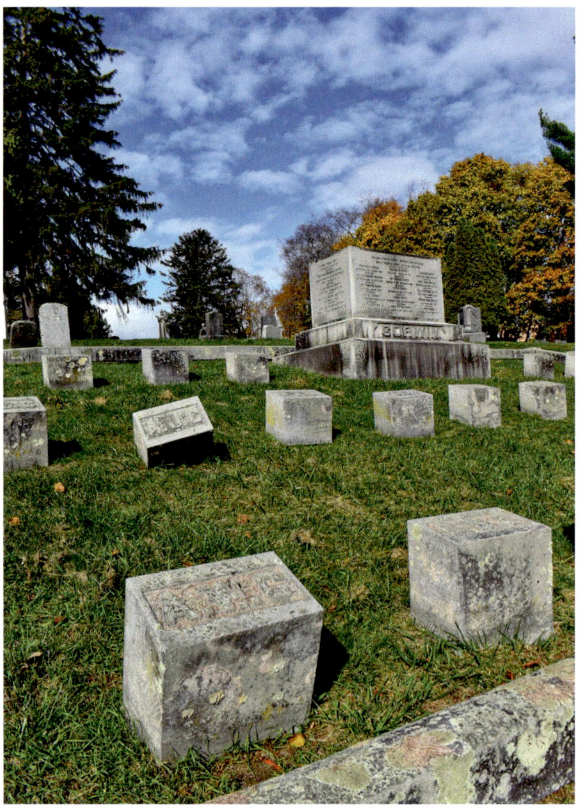

The large Corwin plot, where the Hartfords are buried, consists of many individual headstones and graves.

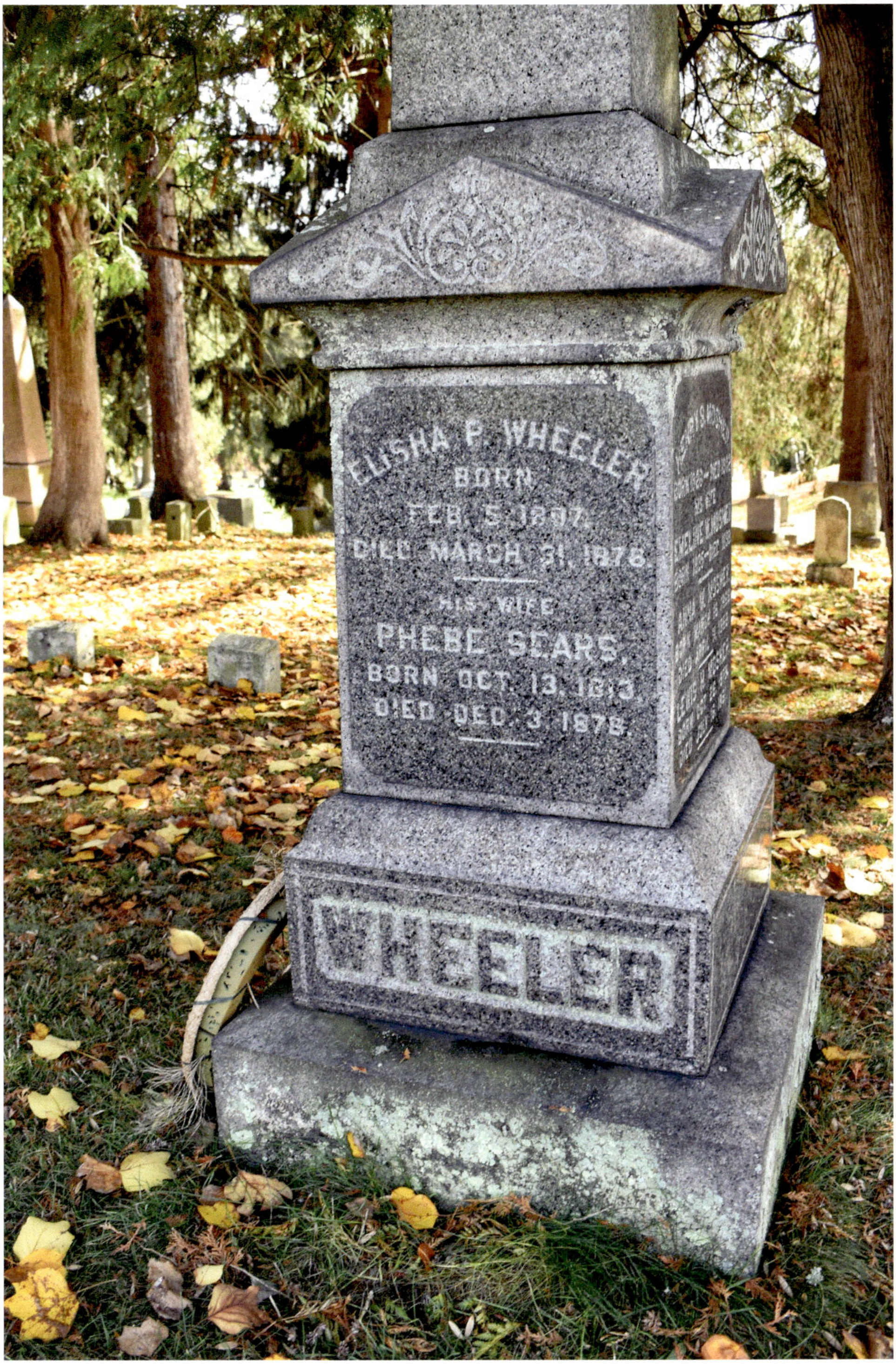

The unassuming grave of E. P. Wheeler is nestled in a shady area of the cemetery.

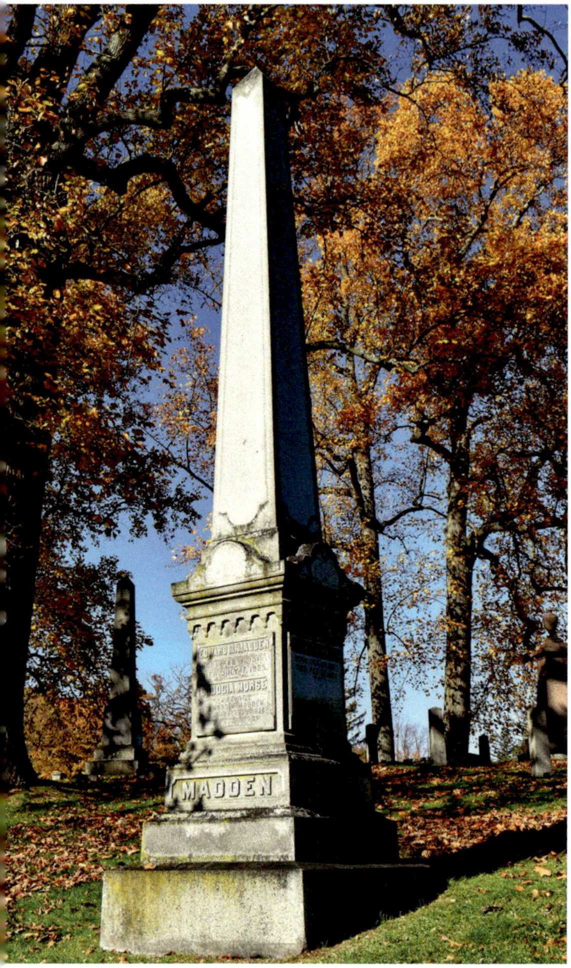

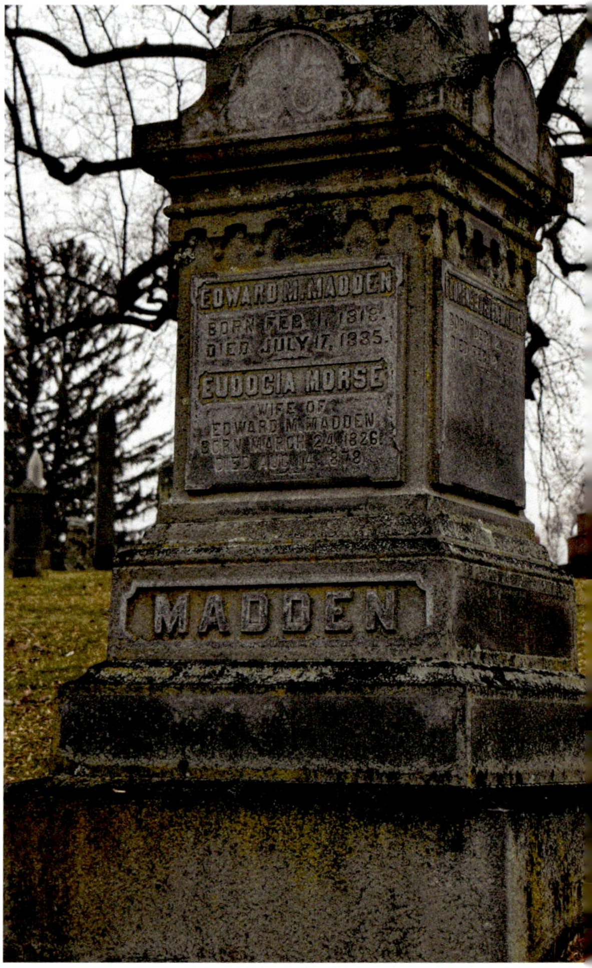

E. M. Madden was a runaway at age nine. Despite his unfortunate beginnings, he was a successful businessman and politician.

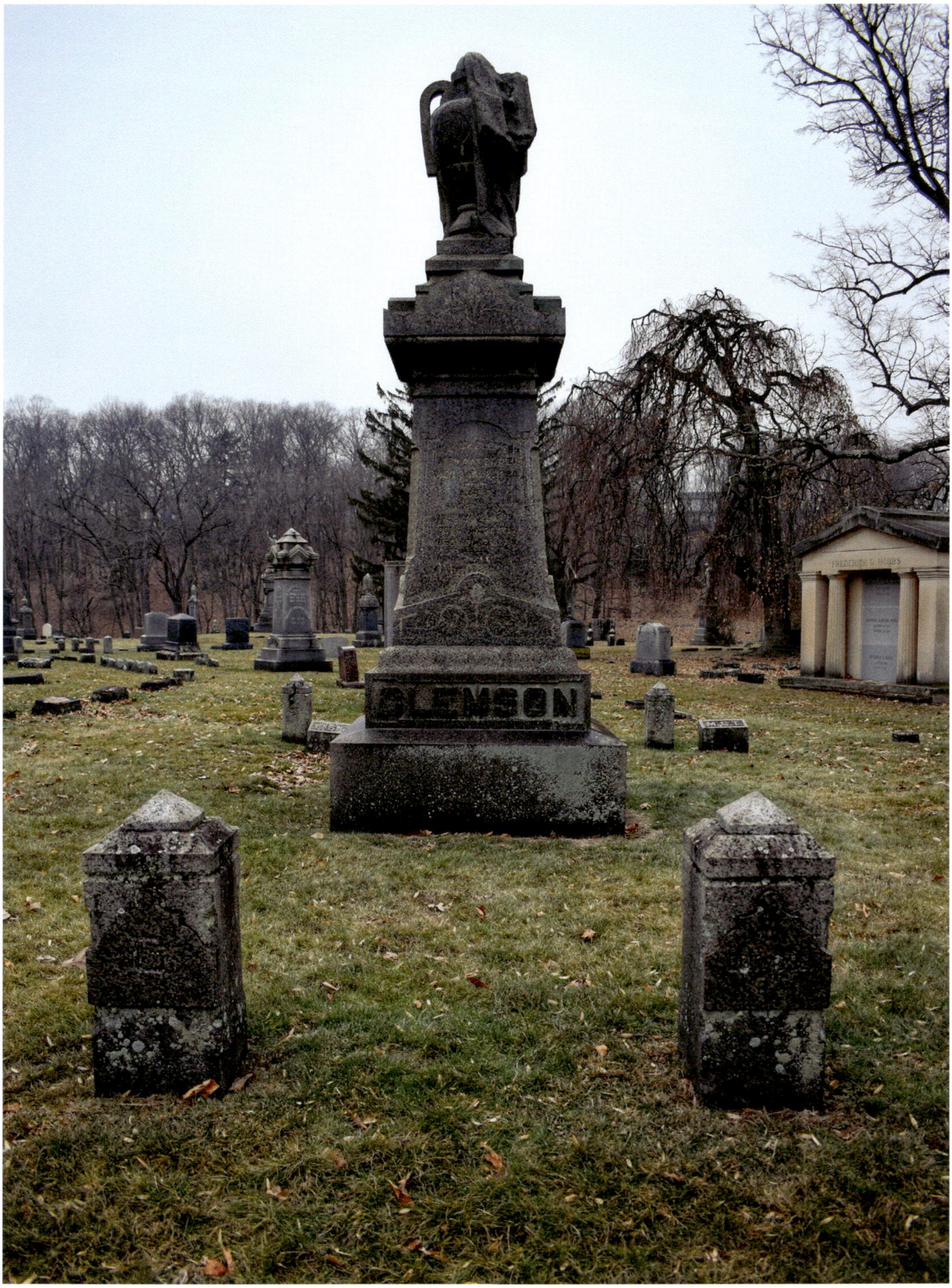

The William Clemson monument has a draped urn embellishing the top.

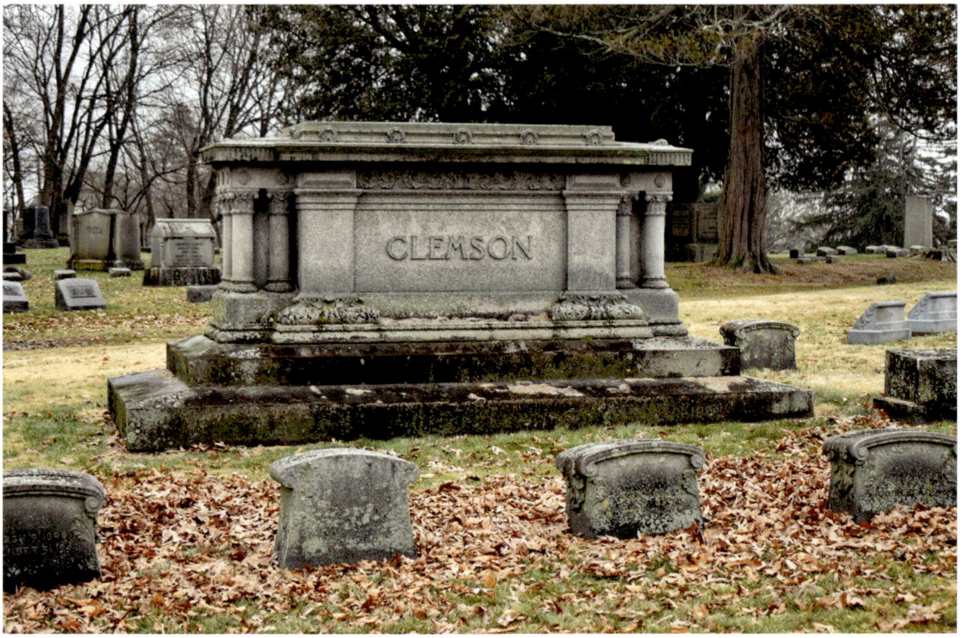

The George N. Clemson family plot includes members of the Schrade and Cross families.

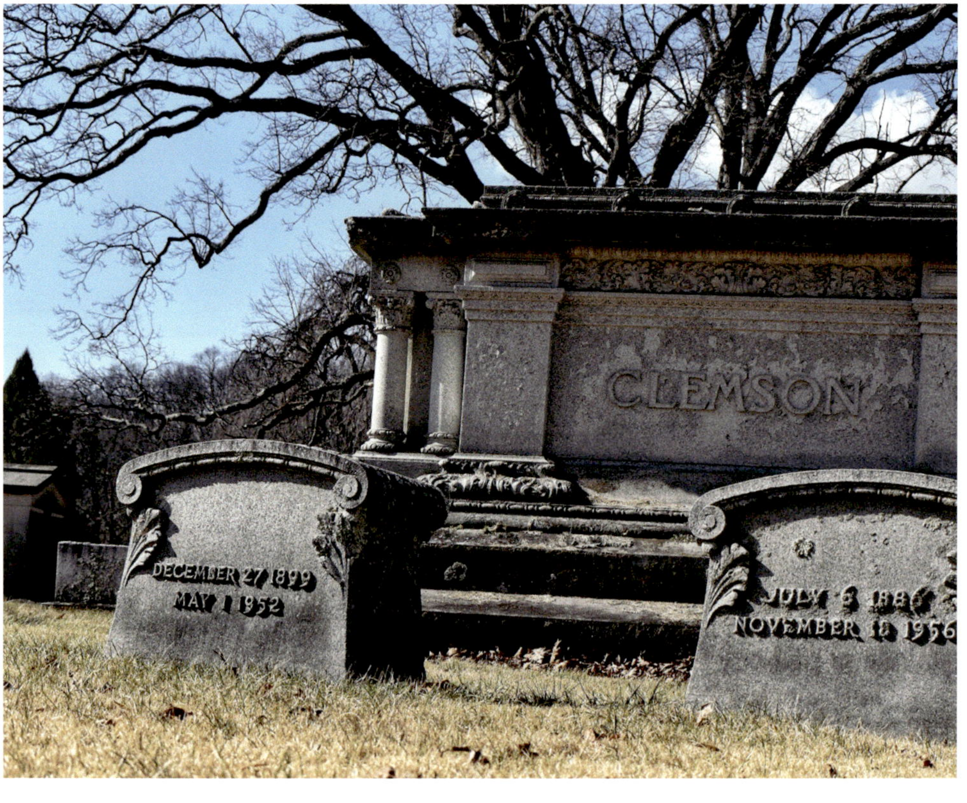

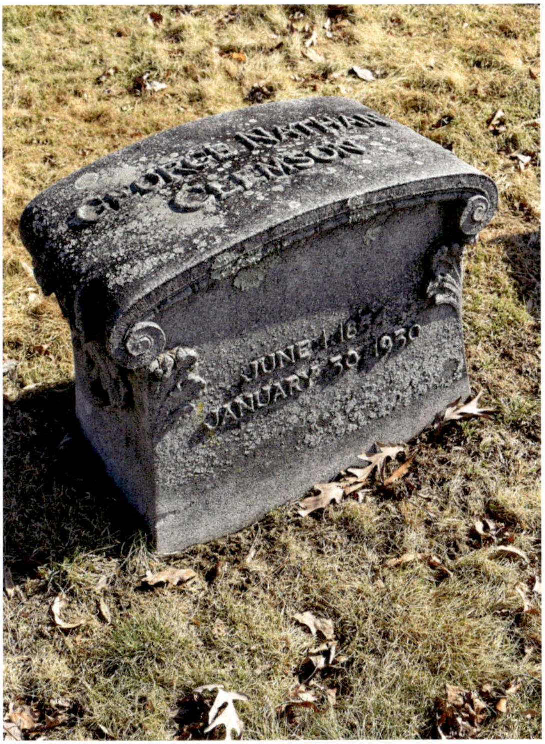

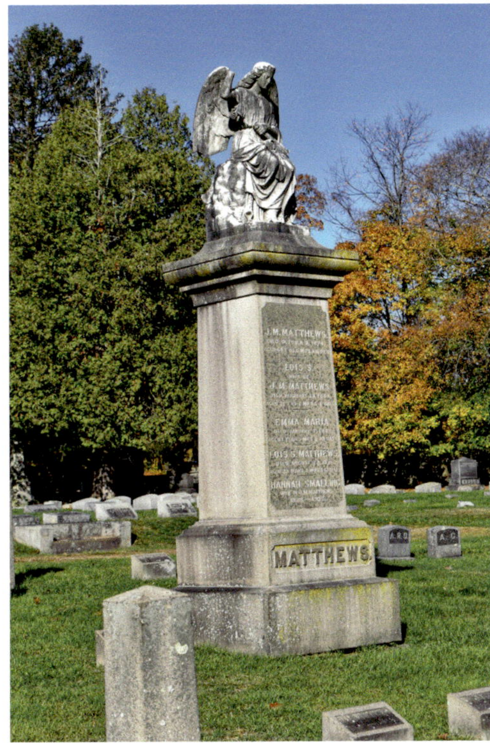

Above left: George N. Clemson, inventor and businessman, is laid to rest here with his family.

Above right: J. M. Matthews owned a carpetbag factory in the mid-1800s with H. H. Hunt on the corner of North and Roberts Streets in downtown Middletown.

Right: The elegance of the Matthews angel is accentuated under the vivid blue sky.

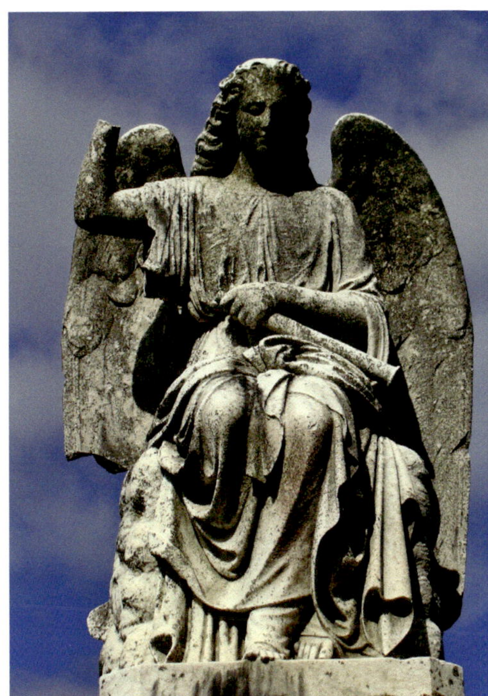

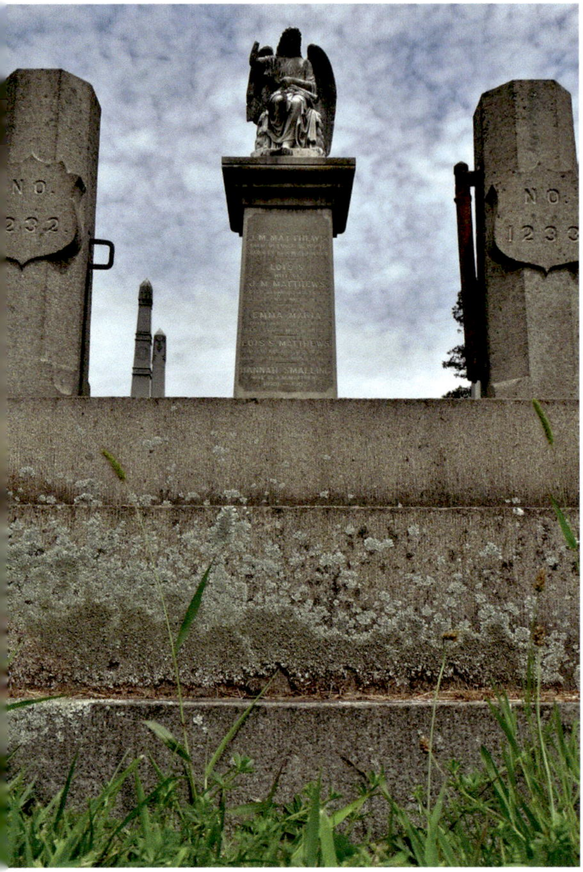

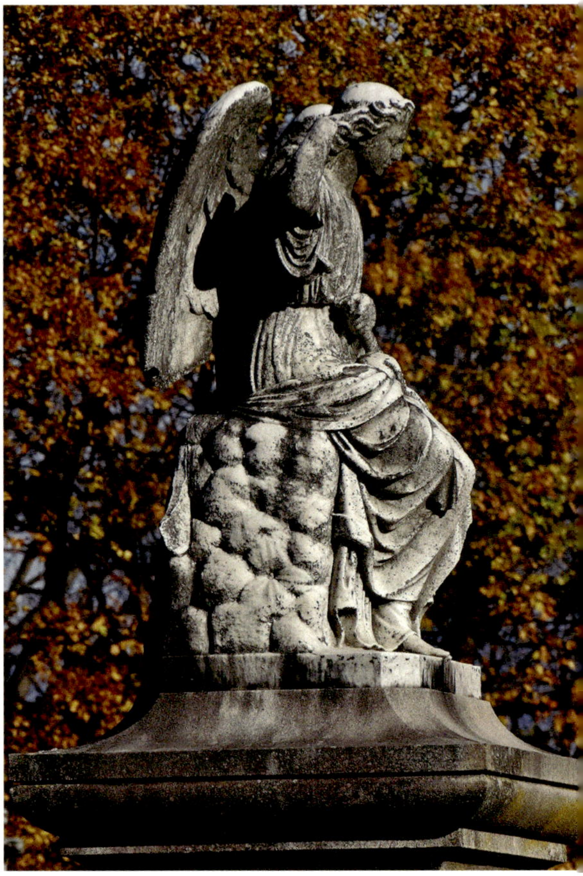

Above left: The steps that lead into the Matthews plot appear to once have had a gate.

Above right: Although she is missing a hand and a wing tip, the Matthews angel is a celestial beauty.

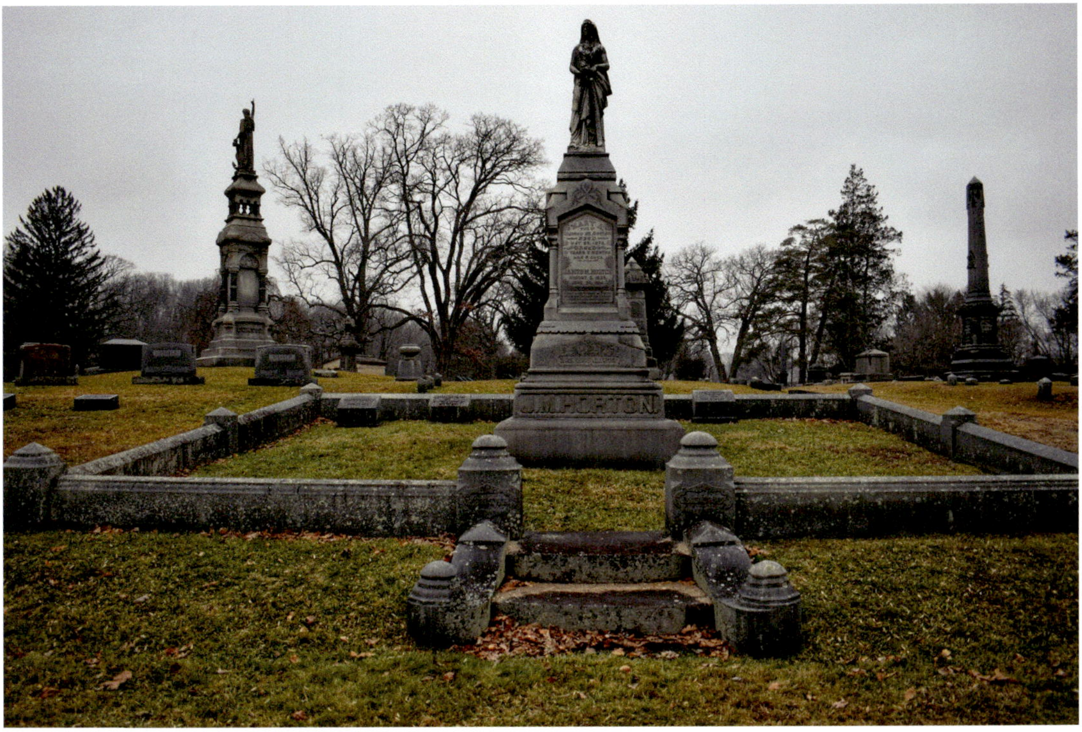

J. M. Horton was the founder of Horton's Ice Cream.

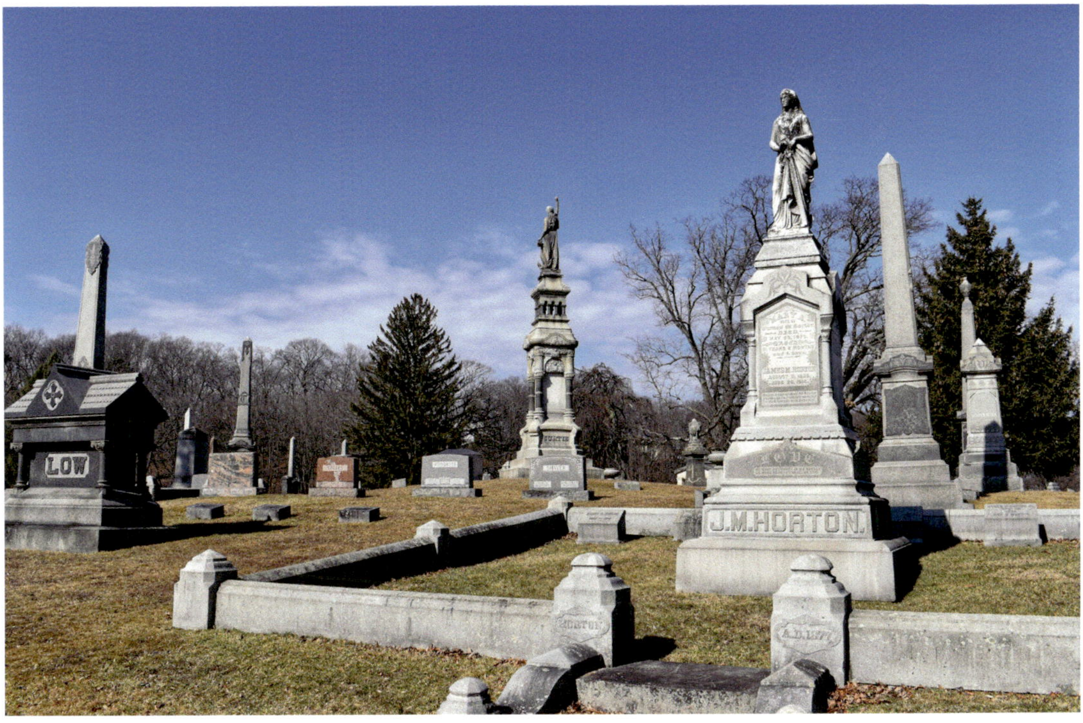

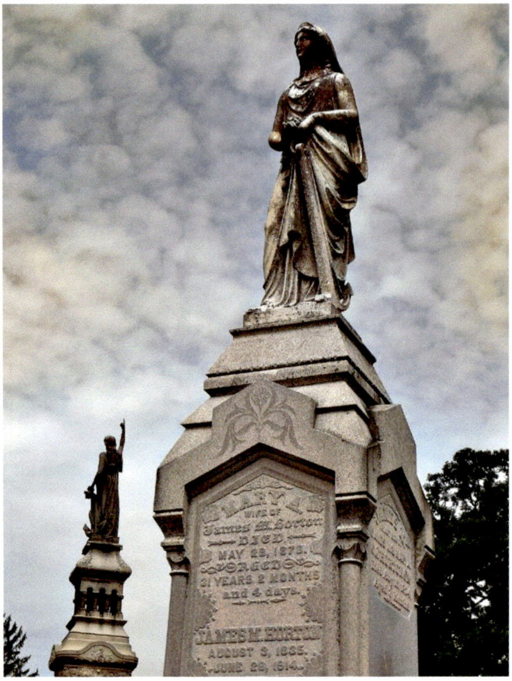

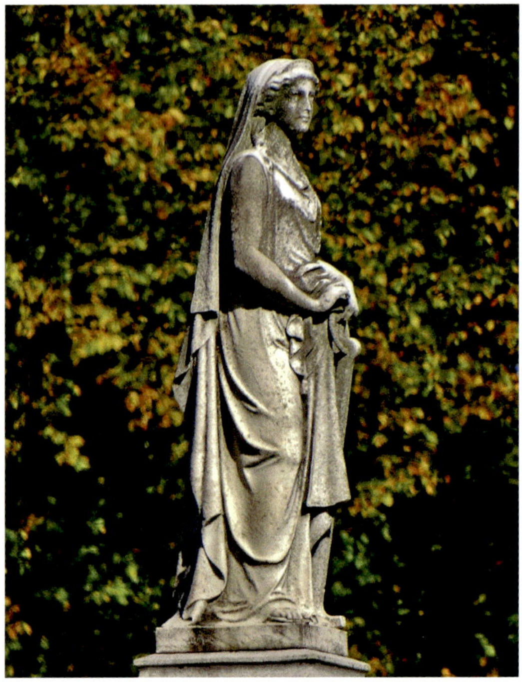

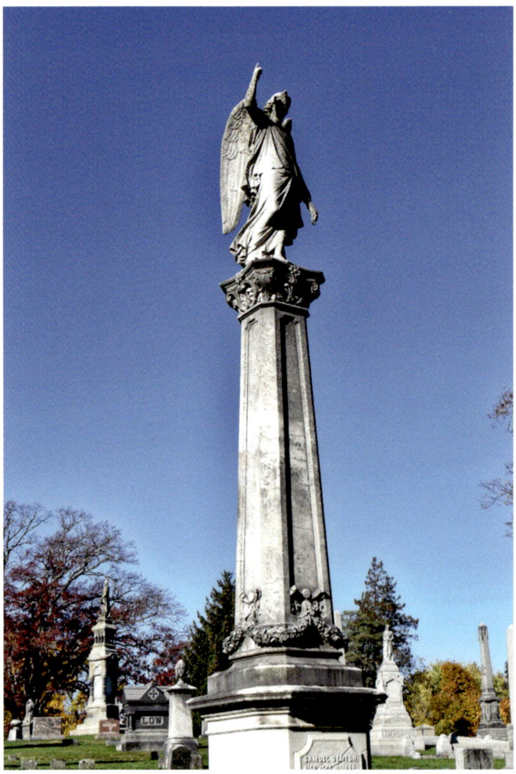

Above left: J. M. Horton's monument has an inscription that states: "Hope—he that believeth in me though he were dead yet shall he live."

Above right: J. M. Horton's statue also symbolizes hope; the figure has an anchor at her feet.

Left: Longtime storekeeper Samuel Denton's family memorial is another masterpiece in Hillside.

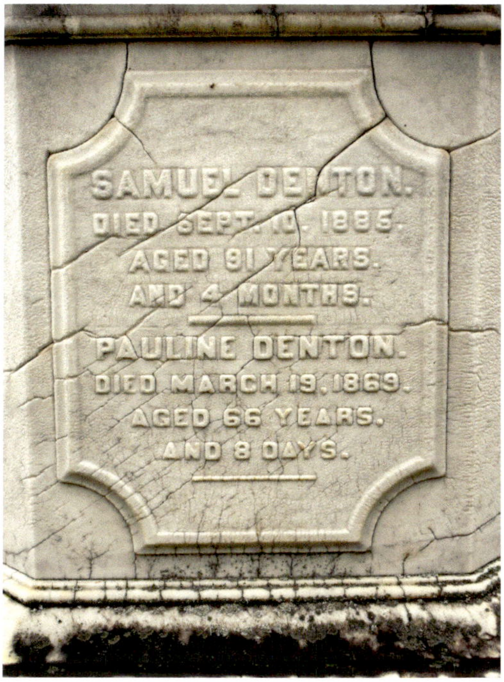

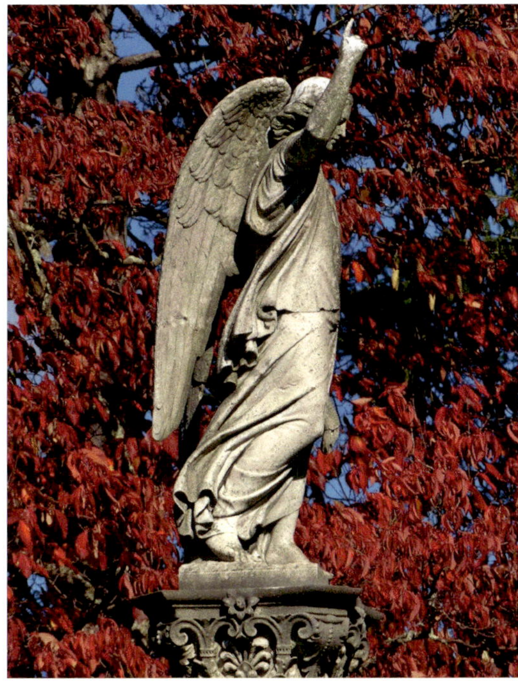

Above left: Despite some interesting cracking patterns, the epitaph on the Denton stone is unusually legible.

Above right: Scarlet leaves provide a fiery backdrop for Samuel Denton's monument.

Right: Denton's angel points to the storm clouds in a sea of obelisks.

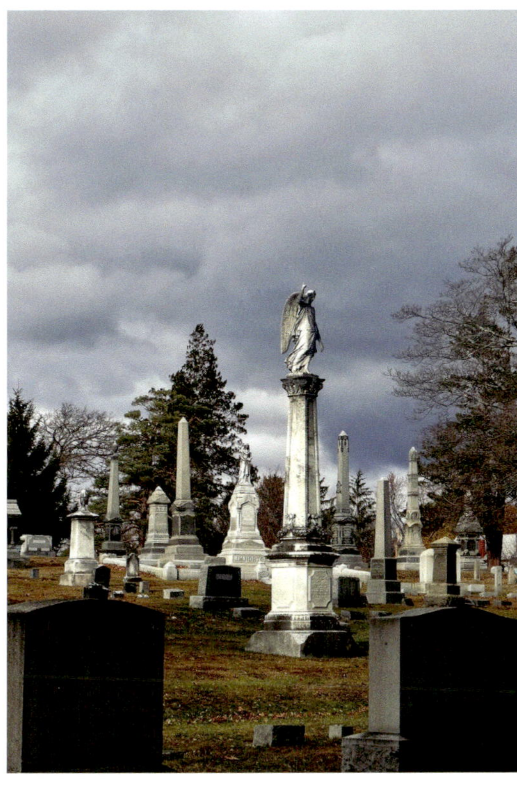

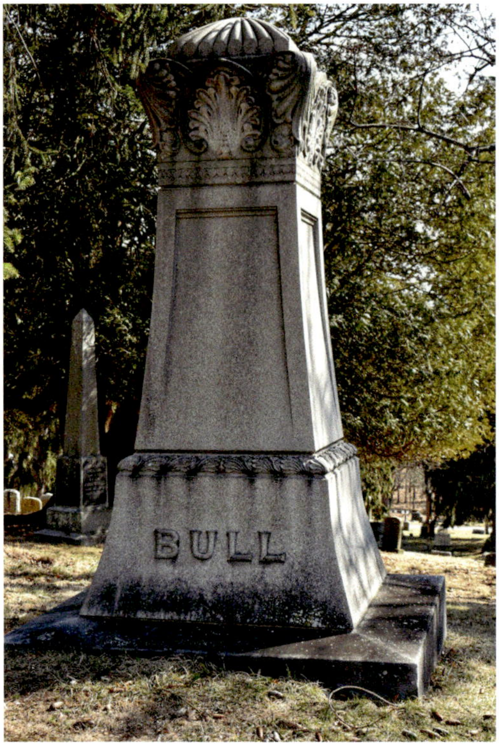

Albert Bull opened Bull's Opera House, Middletown's first theater, in 1871.

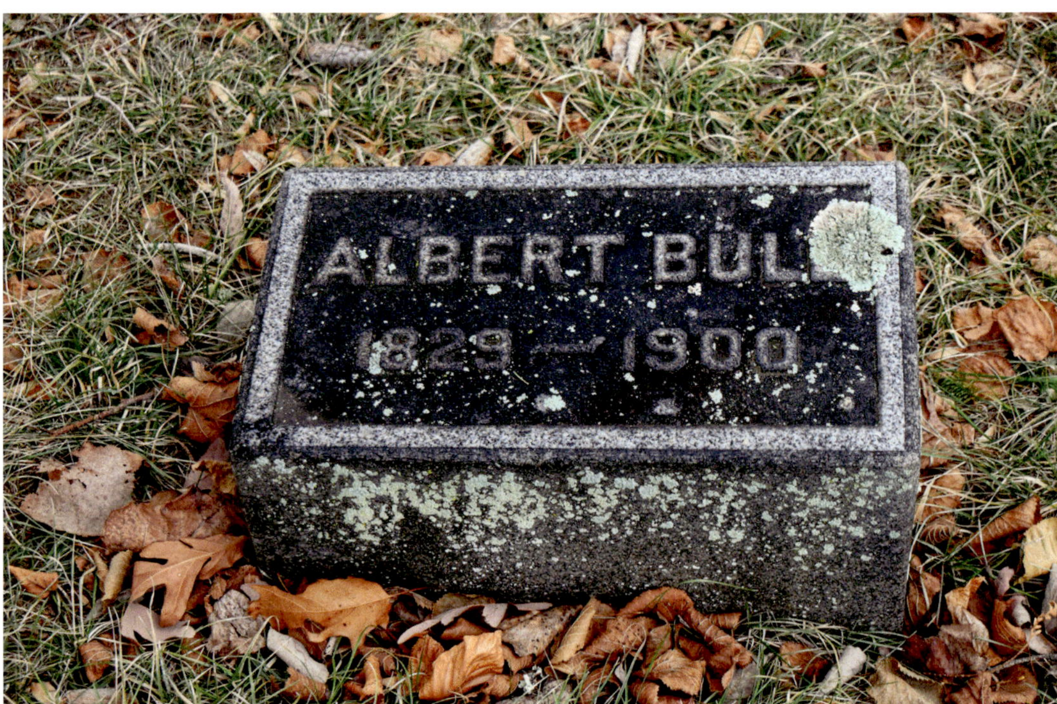

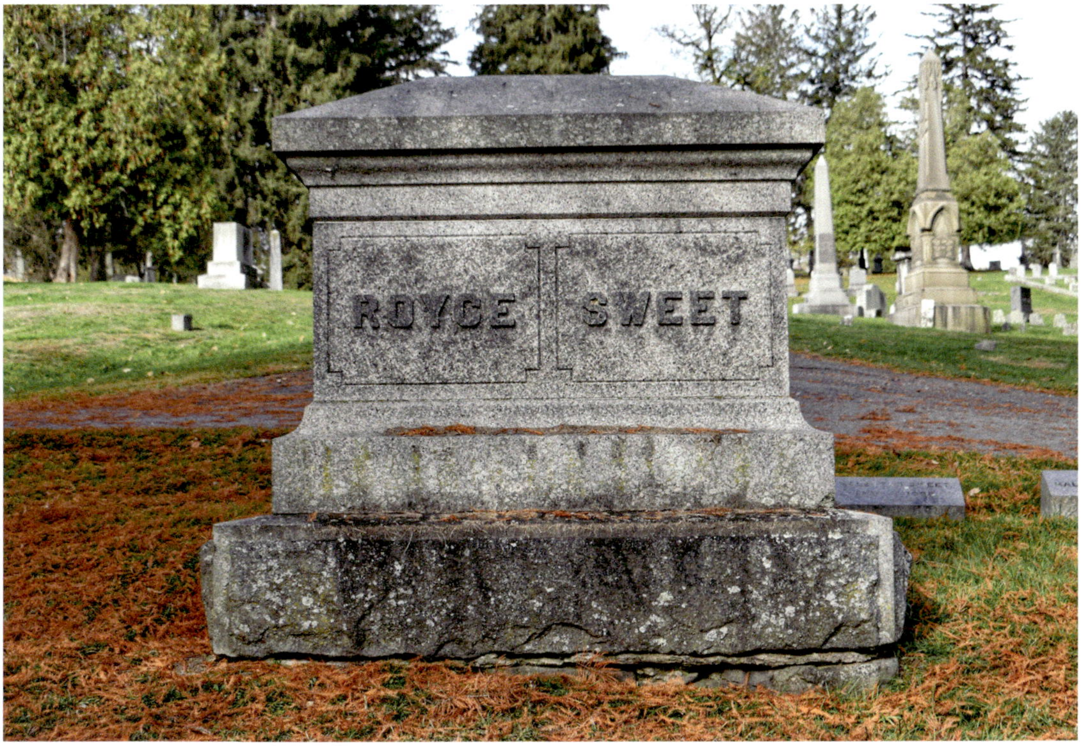

Halstead Sweet owned the popular Sweet's Hotel and enjoyed dabbling in politics.

6

Newsworthy Burials of Hillside

Whether it was the way a person lived, the manner in which they died, or sometimes both, there are some interesting burials in Hillside that made headlines due to their fame, misfortune, or tragic deaths.

Eleanor Merron Cowper (1867–1908) and James H. Wallick (1839–1908) were two actors that had a suicide pact. Wallick was an orphan, born Patrick Fubbins in Middletown, and was adopted by the Wheeler family. He was then known as Hank Wheeler, later acquiring his stage name of James Wallick. After a successful career as an actor and producer, he ran into financial and health trouble. On May 1, 1908, he shot himself in a hotel room in Middletown and died. Eleanor, also an actor and playwright, worked with Wallick on *The Dairy Farm*. Her earnings from that play enabled her to build a home in Middletown. She had been married to Archibald "Archie" Cowper (1852–1906), and after his death, continued a friendship with Wallick. On December 2, 1908, Eleanor shot herself in a New York City hotel, also ending her life. It was later revealed through letters that Eleanor had written to her attorney that she had purposely waited to commit suicide to not interfere with Wallick's burial. When Wallick died first, Eleanor read poetry at his grave. Wallick and his wife, Mary (1848–1898), are buried alongside Eleanor and Archie in the Wallick family plot.

John E. Minshull (1849–1879) was a master mechanic for the Midland Railroad. He lost his life jumping from a steam car to avoid a collision during a routine railroad inspection. His large gravestone in Hillside is a tribute to how respected and admired Minshull was, in his chosen field and as a man. The inscription reads: "Erected by his fellow officers and laborers as an expression of their regard for the manliness, integrity and generosity of his character, and of their deep affection for one whose aim it was to know and do the right."

Alice Zane Grey (1839–1917) was the mother of author Zane Grey. He lived in Middletown for a couple years, buying his mother a house in town on South Street. The house has since been demolished. Alice is buried here alone under an evergreen tree.

Alice Ingerick (d. in 1905) was only nine years old when she died. Her mother, Georgia, worked as a housekeeper for Frederick and Willis Olney, who had a farm on the outskirts of town. In October 1905, little Alice and the Olney brothers were found murdered on the farm. Georgia was attacked as well, but she lived. Despite her injuries, authorities were trying to work with her to solve the murders. In her weakened state, she named several potential suspects to no avail. Eventually, in 1907, evidence pointed to a man named Charles Rogers. He was apprehended and arrested in California for the murders. Rogers was tried and put to death in July 1908.

Lancelot "Launt" Thompson (1833–1894) was a sculptor born in Ireland. He arrived in Albany, New York, in 1847, and became an assistant to sculptor Erastus Dow Palmer. Originally, he had hoped to become a doctor and his study of anatomy proved to be useful in his art career. In 1857, he opened his own studio in New York City. In 1871, at the height of his career, he moved to Italy with his wife, Mary; however, Thompson returned back to the city by himself in 1881. Sadly, the years that followed were a downward spiral for him, as he had developed alcoholism. He died at the Middletown State Hospital. Actor Edwin Booth helped pay for some of Thompson's expenses at the asylum, but no one attended his funeral and his grave in Hillside was reportedly unmarked for a long time. Despite his unfortunate demise, Thompson's legacy lives on through his work, having sculptures displayed at the Smithsonian and the Metropolitan Museum of Art, as well as in Washington, DC, and West Point. At Burnside Park in Rhode Island, Thompson's equestrian sculpture of Ambrose Burnside, a Civil War general and former governor of Rhode Island, graces the center of the park.

Amelia J. Goldsmith Gregory (1840–1891) was a wife to Noah and mother of two boys. The Gregory family had a celery farm just outside the Middletown city limits. In October 1891, while her husband and older son were out working in the fields, Amelia was viciously murdered in her home, only to be discovered by her youngest son when he returned home from school. After a sensational investigation and trial, one of the farmhands, Fred Maguire, was found to be guilty of Amelia's murder. Fred's "gang", including his live-in girlfriend, Sarah, and another of Noah Gregory's farm hands named Warren Brazington, pointed the finger at each other for the crime. Although Sarah and Warren were charged with being accessories, Maguire went to the electric chair for Amelia's murder in 1892. Sadly, robbery was the motive; $100 was stolen from the Gregory home on the day of the murder. Amelia is buried in the Goldsmith family plot in Hillside.

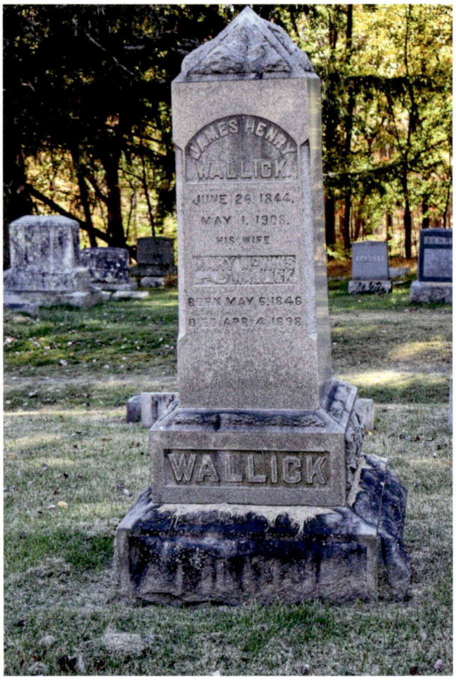

Left: The monument in the James Wallick plot has an inscription on its right side: "Then are they glad because they are at rest: And so he bringeth them unto the haven where they would be."

Below: The grave of Eleanor Cowper is in the Wallick plot.

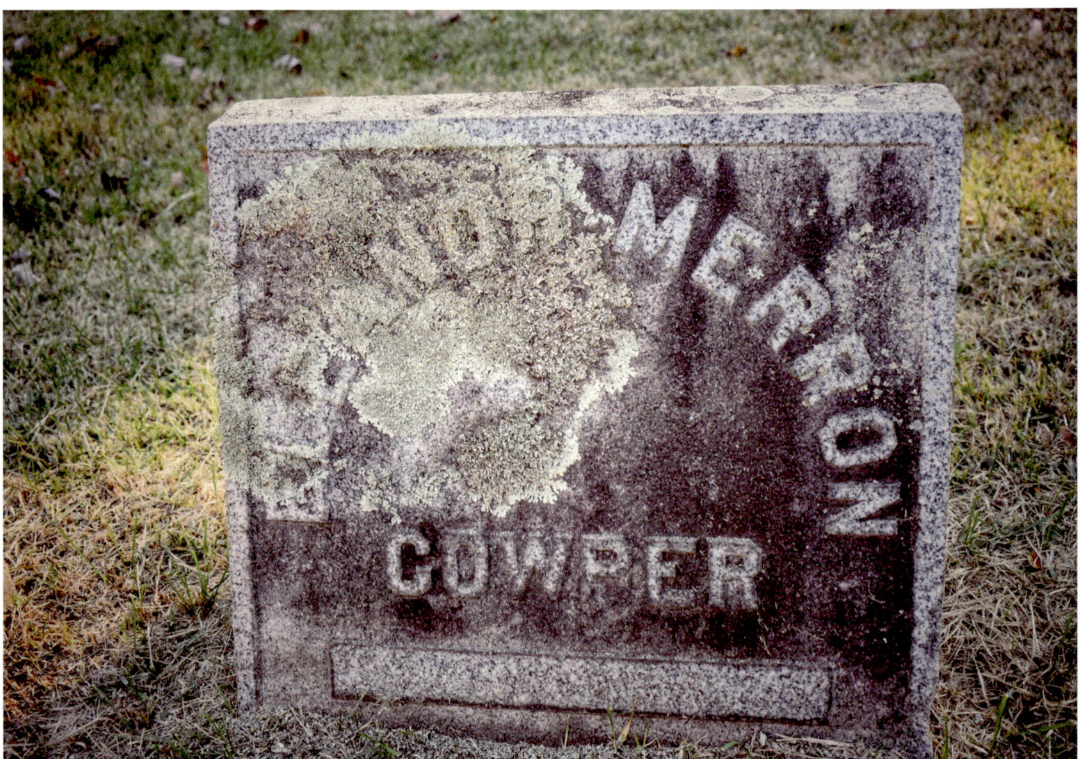

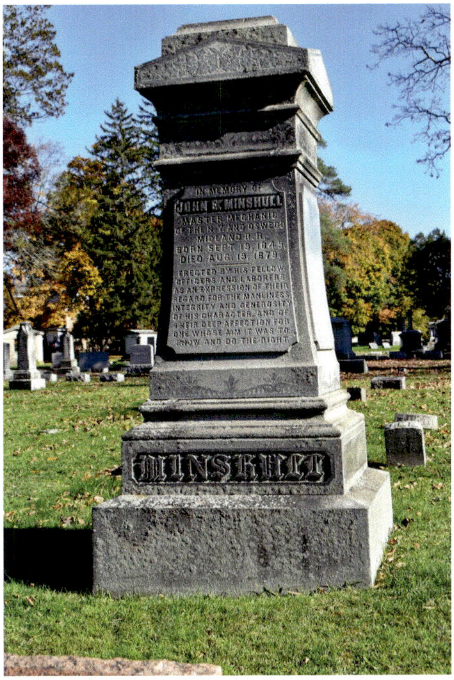

Right: John Minshull's tragic death saddened an entire community.

Below: Alice Grey is buried alone in Hillside.

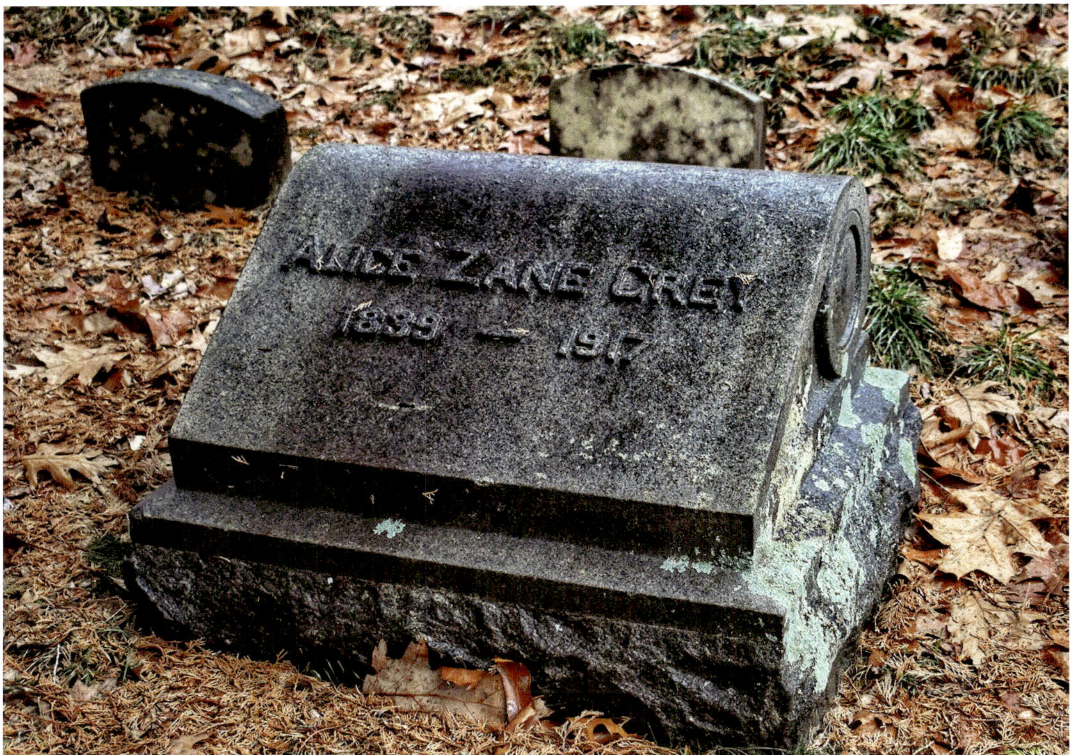

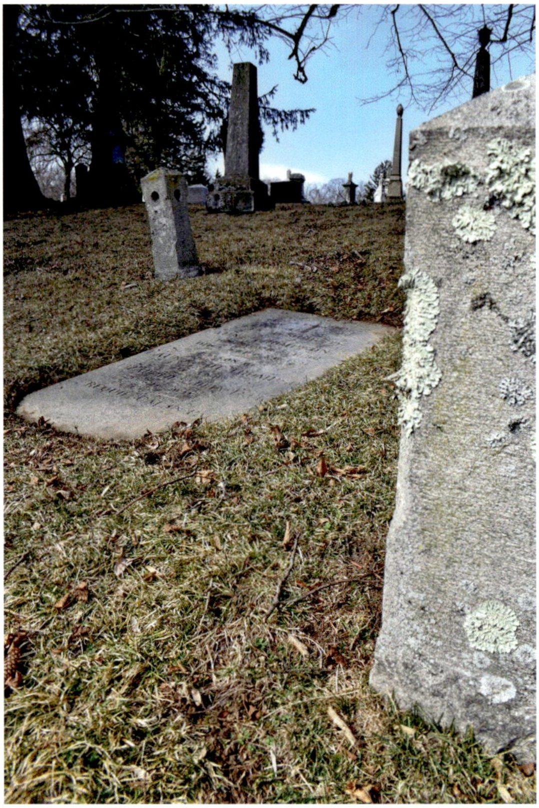

The grave of artist Launt Thompson was reported to be unmarked. He was a successful sculptor, and then his life took a devastating turn.

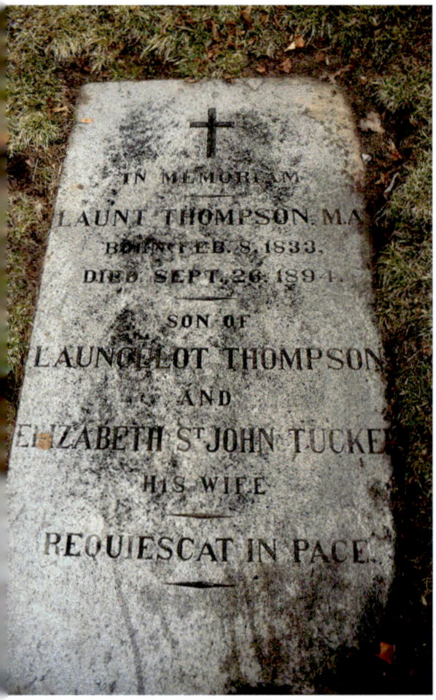

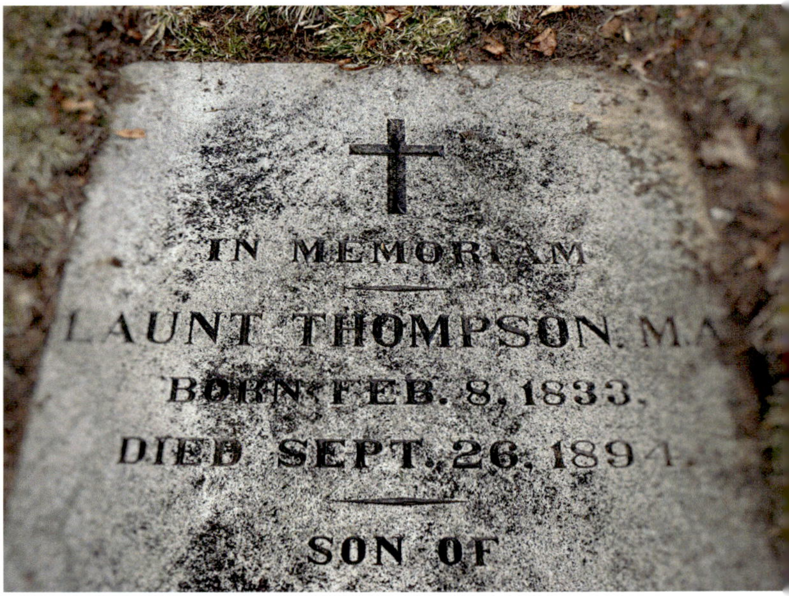

Launt Thompson's poignant memorial is engraved with *Requiescat in Pace*.

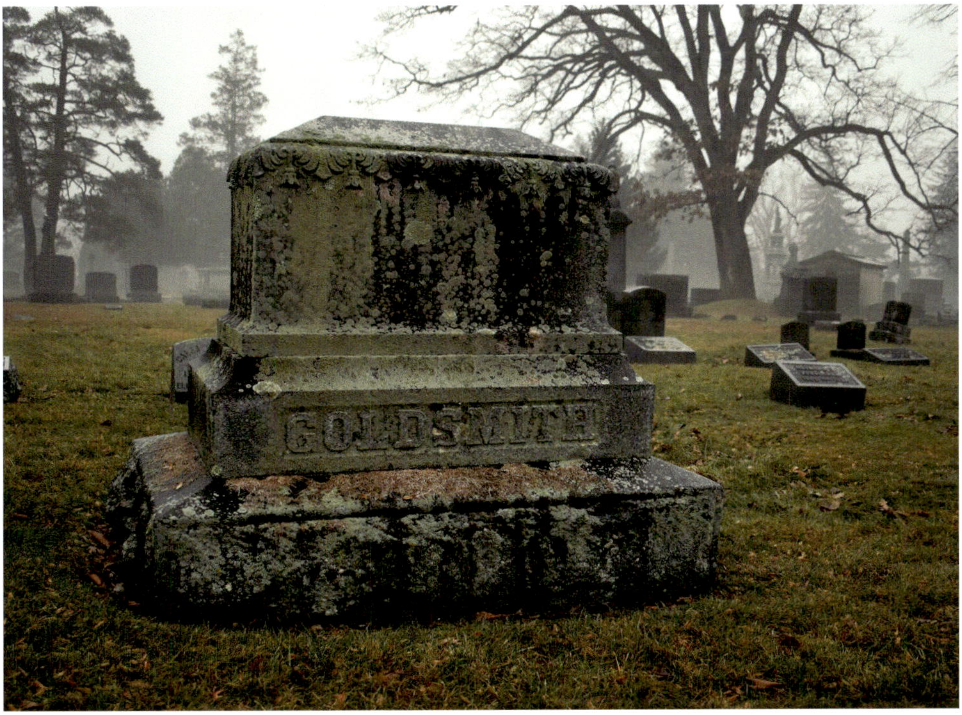

Amelia Goldsmith Gregory was buried in the Goldsmith plot after her heinous murder in 1891.

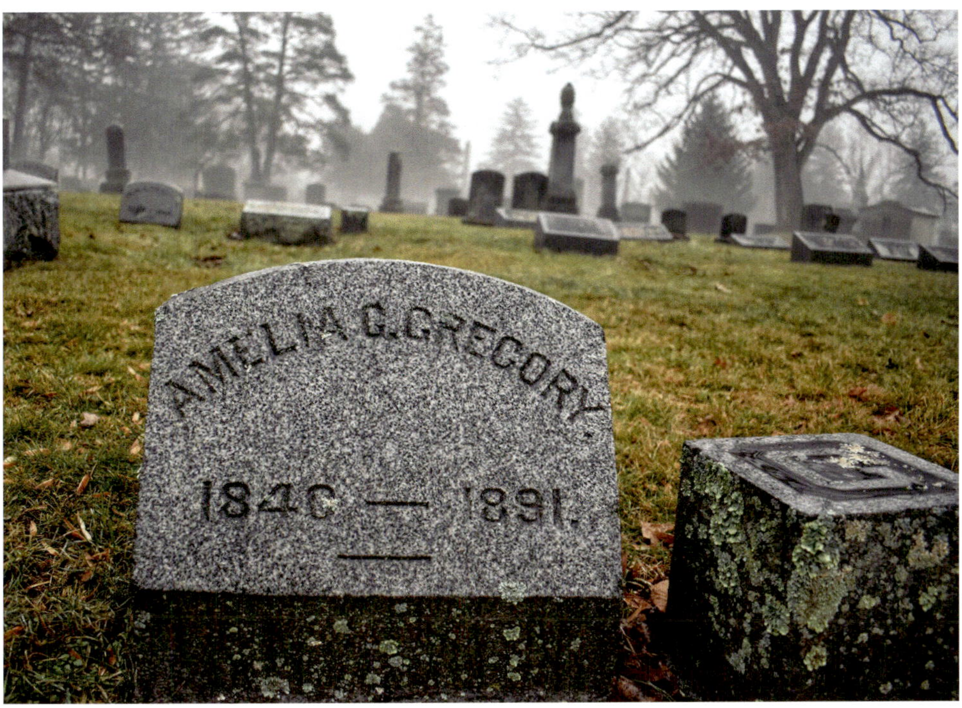

7

Scenes Around Hillside

While Hillside has an enormous historical significance, it is also admired for its aesthetic properties. Some graves are simple and modest, and others are exquisite and grand. Blending Vaux's design, the natural landscape, and the variety of alluring gravestones, Hillside's scenery is truly mesmerizing. The monuments and memorials are both mysterious and revealing.

There's so much more beauty to explore, and there's still so many stories to be told.

Middletown itself and the world around us may change, but Hillside Cemetery is the one constant reminder that history can stay alive if we allow it to. Hillside is truly an American treasure, filled with inspiring and poignant stories of hard work, hope, tragedy, and triumph.

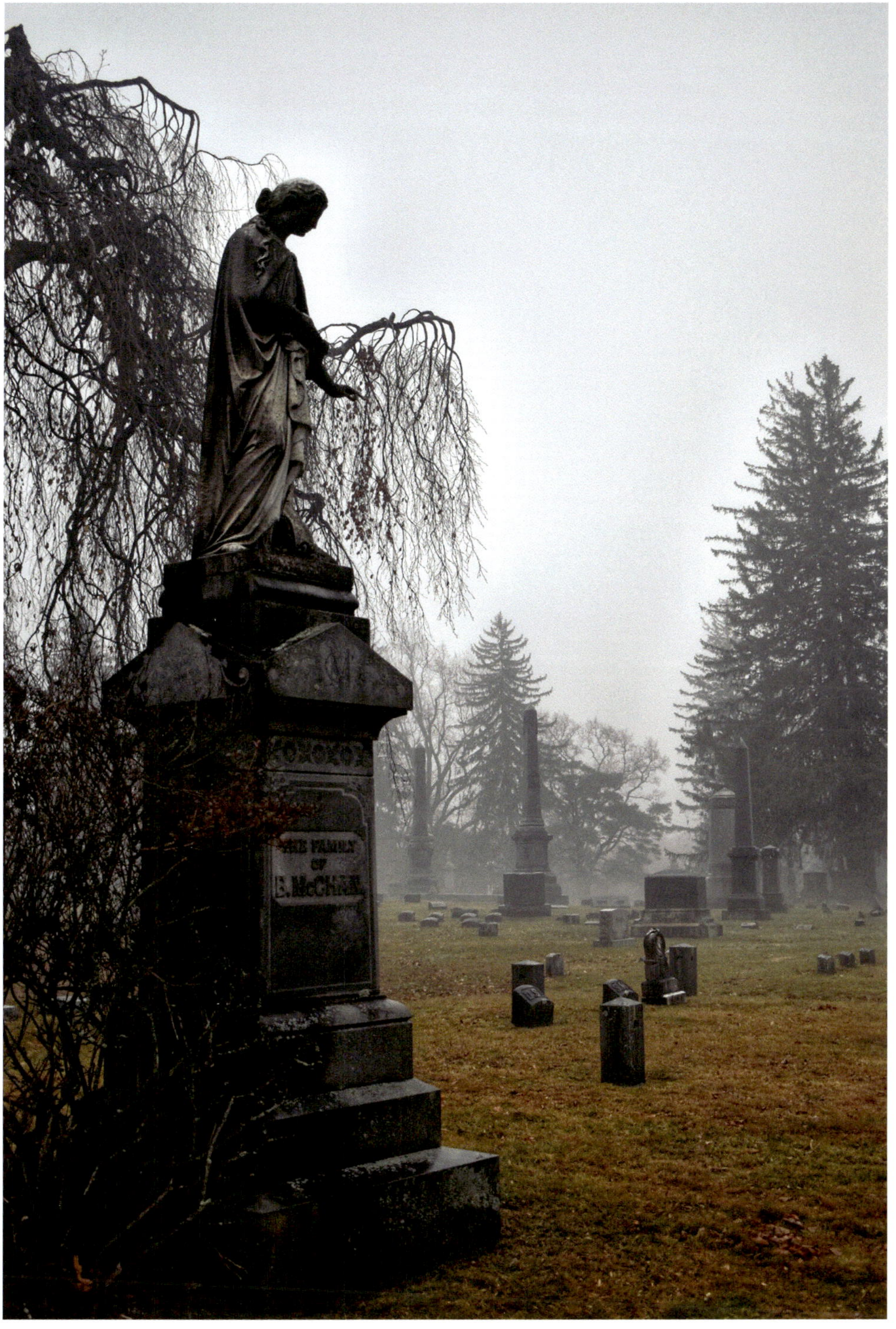

The weeping tree behind the B. McChan monument creates the perfect atmosphere on a foggy day.

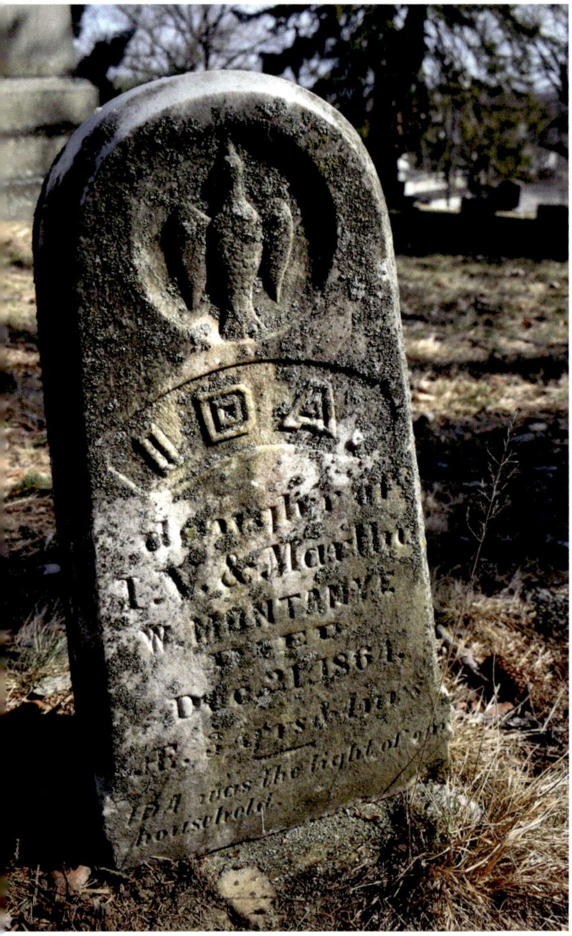

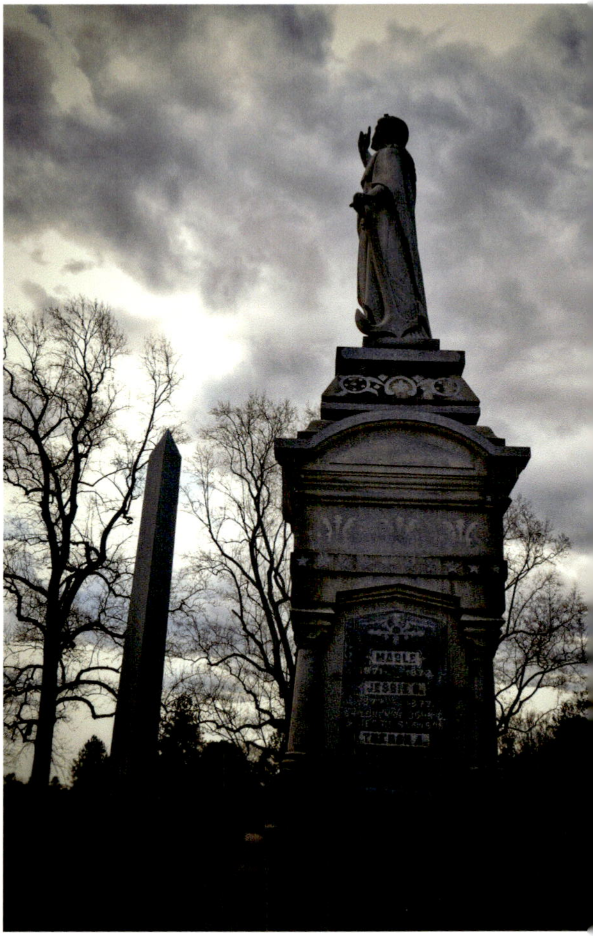

Above left: A beautiful little stone declares that "Ida was the light of our household."

Above right: The ominous skies hang heavily over the Slawson memorial.

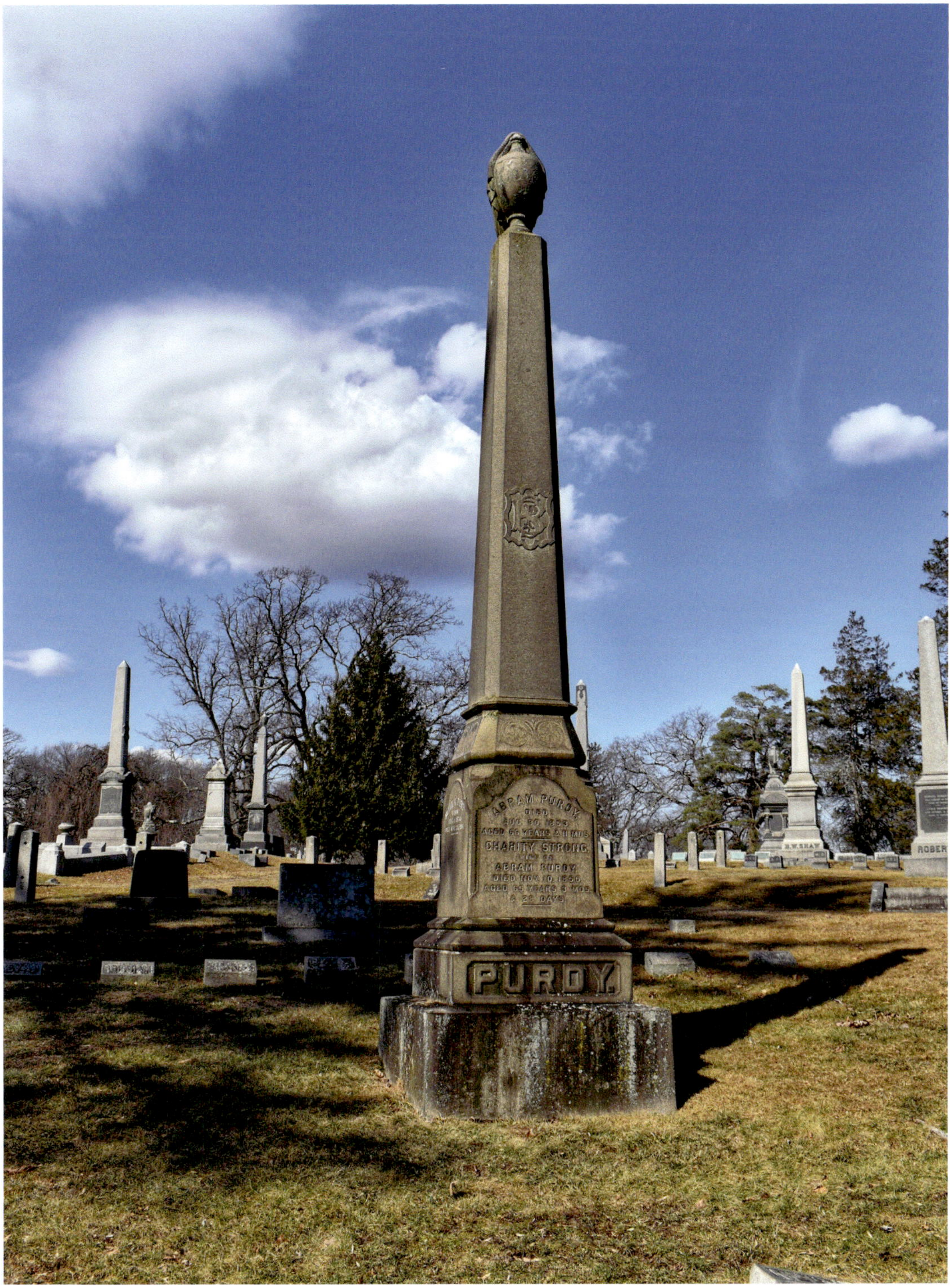

The colors of the Purdy grave compliment the blue sky.

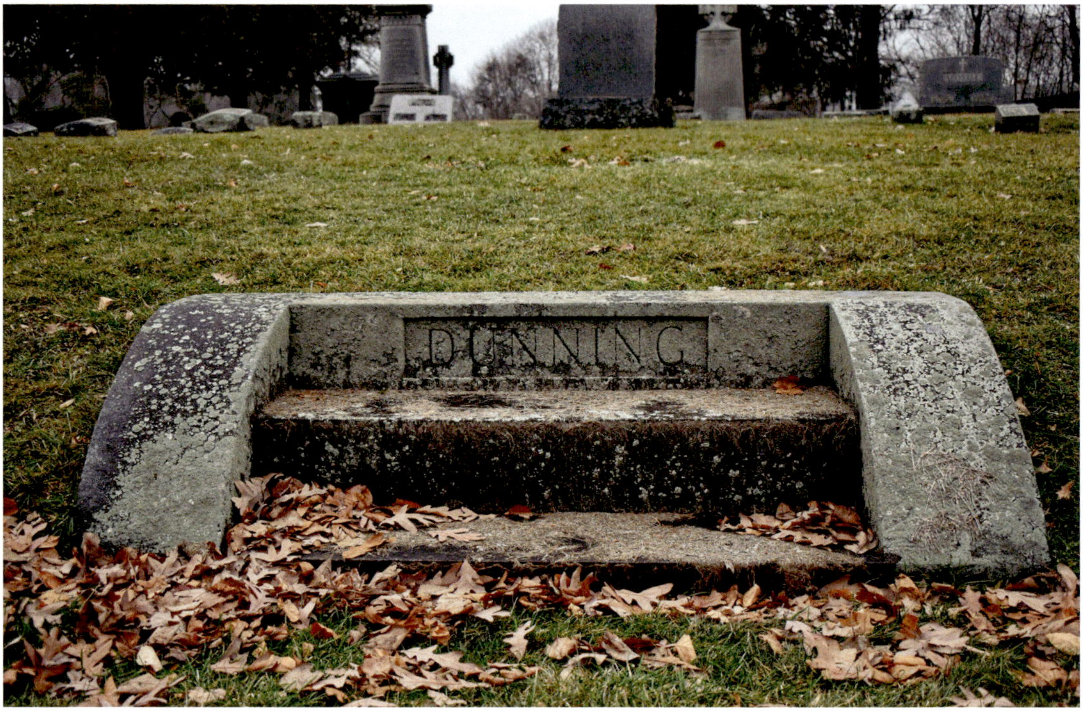

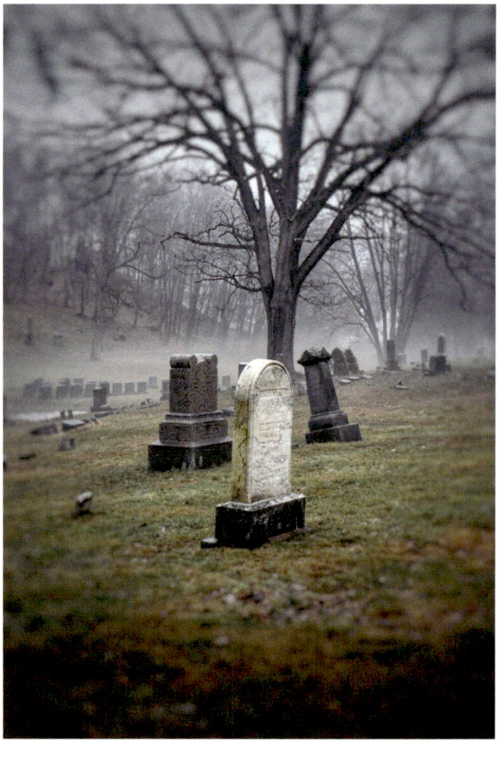

Above: The Dunning family appears to have stairs to nowhere.

Left: Rainy days enhance the colors and the lettering on the tombstones.

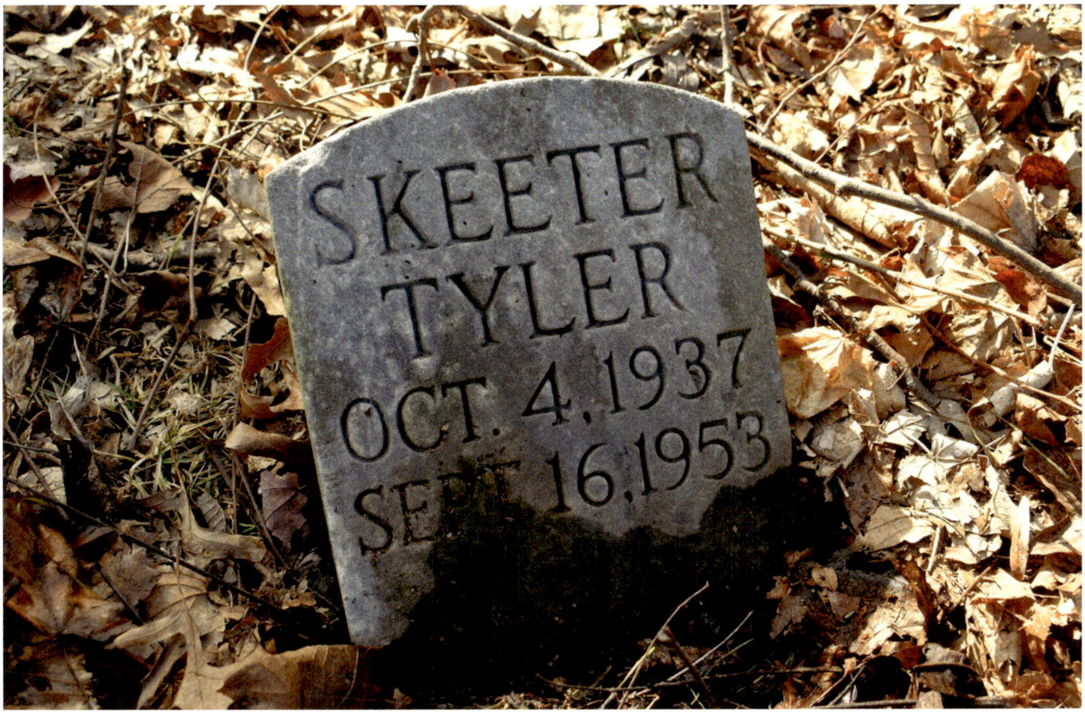

Skeeter Tyler's tidy stone was discovered along the edge of the cemetery.

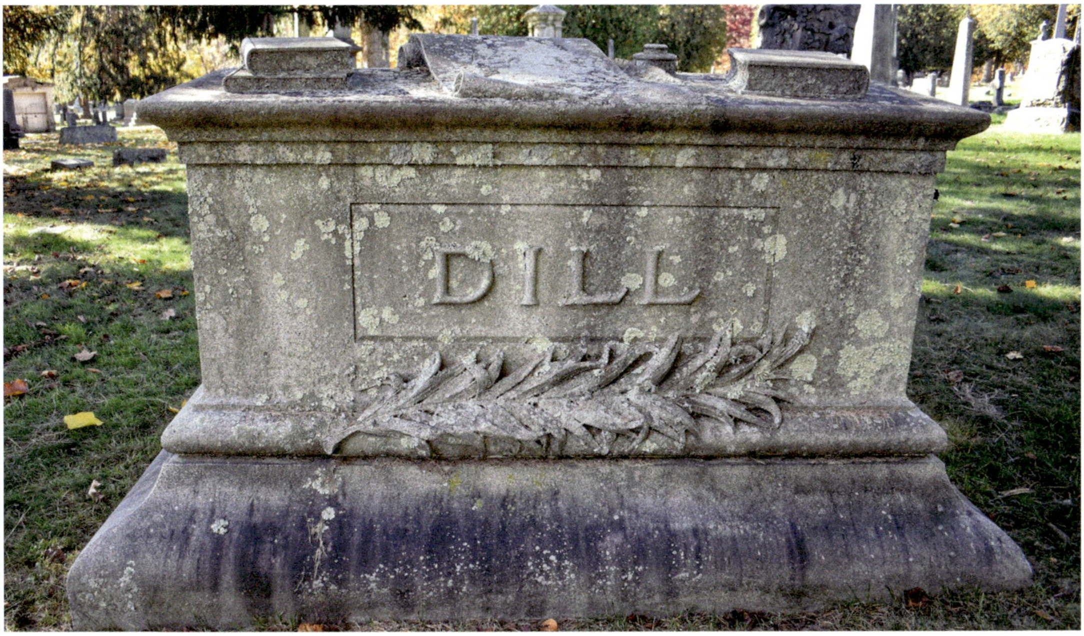

Charles G. Dill (1839–1913) was a Middletown lawyer. His unique monument is a carved desk, complete with a quill pen, an inkwell, books, and a scroll that reads *lax* (Latin for law).

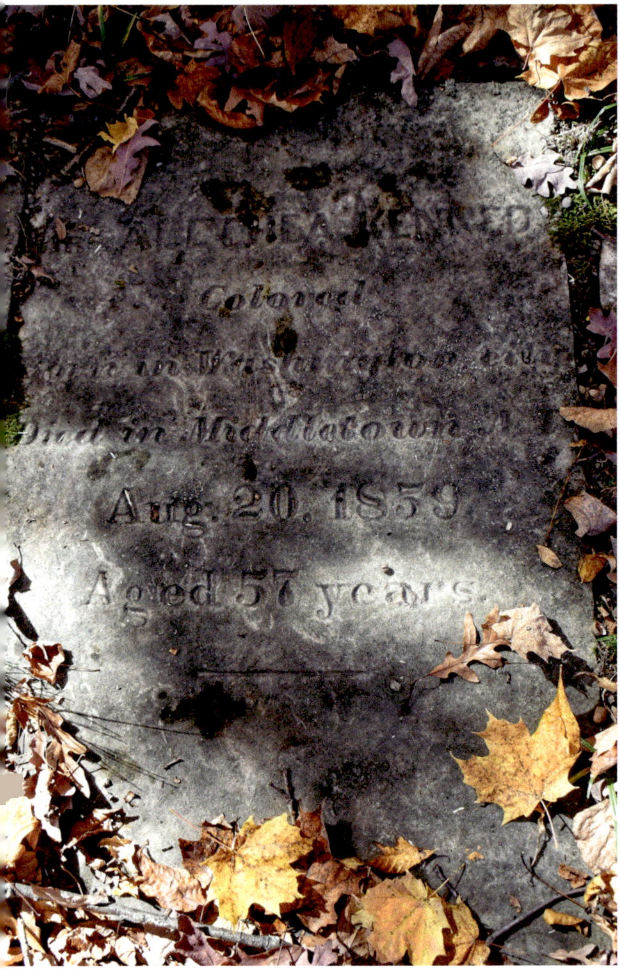

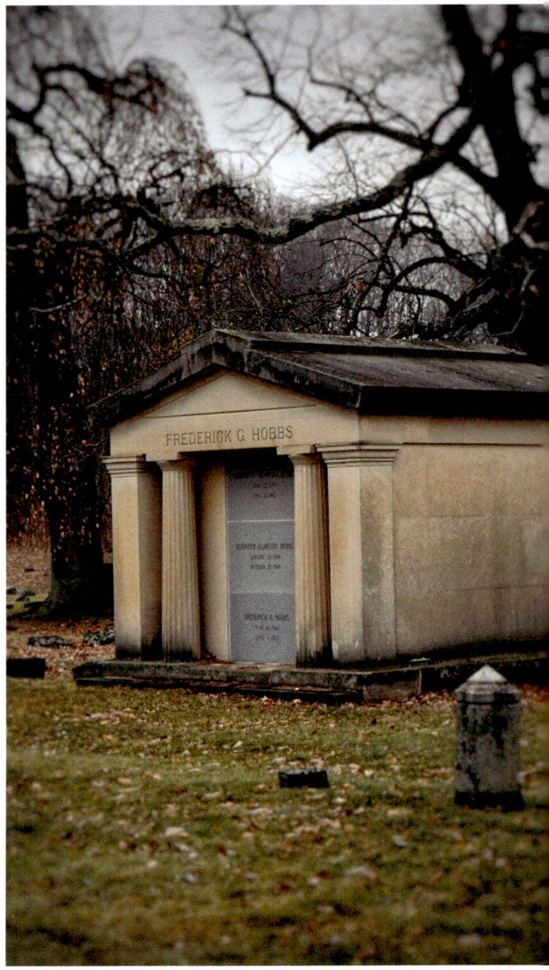

Above left: Althea Kennedy's derogatory epitaph reads: "Colored, born in Washington city." She died in 1859 at fifty-seven years old.

Above right: Frederick G. Hobbs and family are interred in the mausoleum bearing his name.

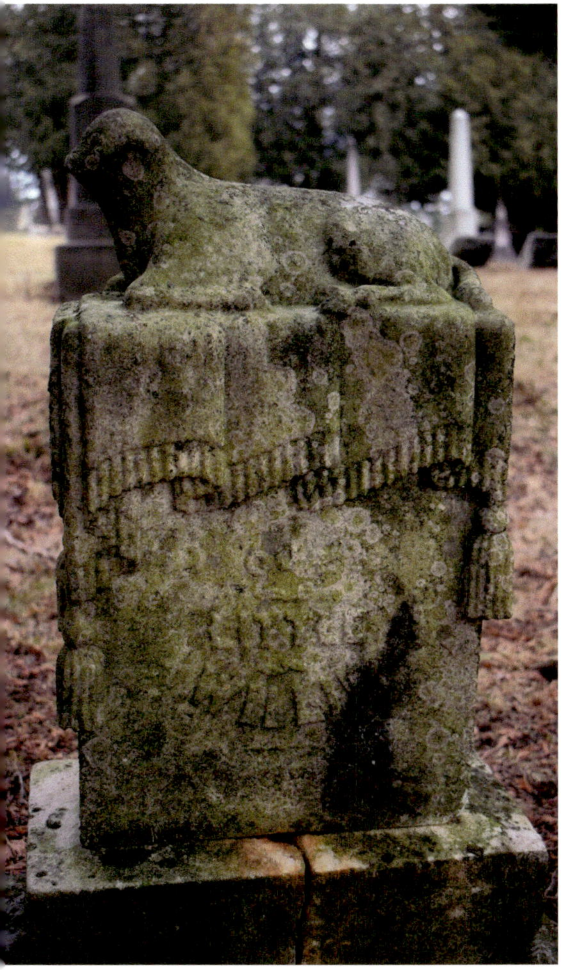

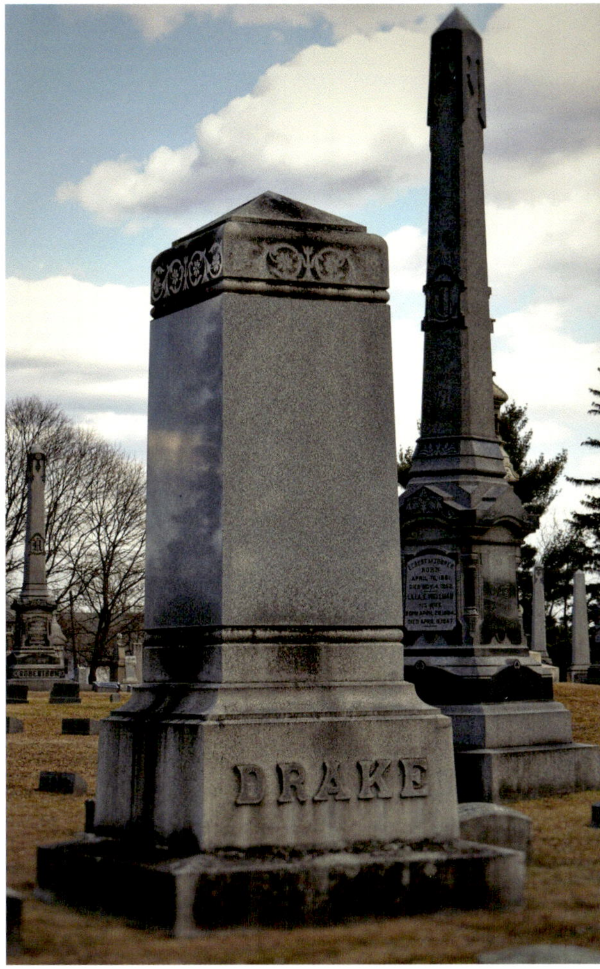

Above left: A tiny stone reads "Our Little Willie."

Above right: The Drake and Tooker families have substantial monuments in Hillside.

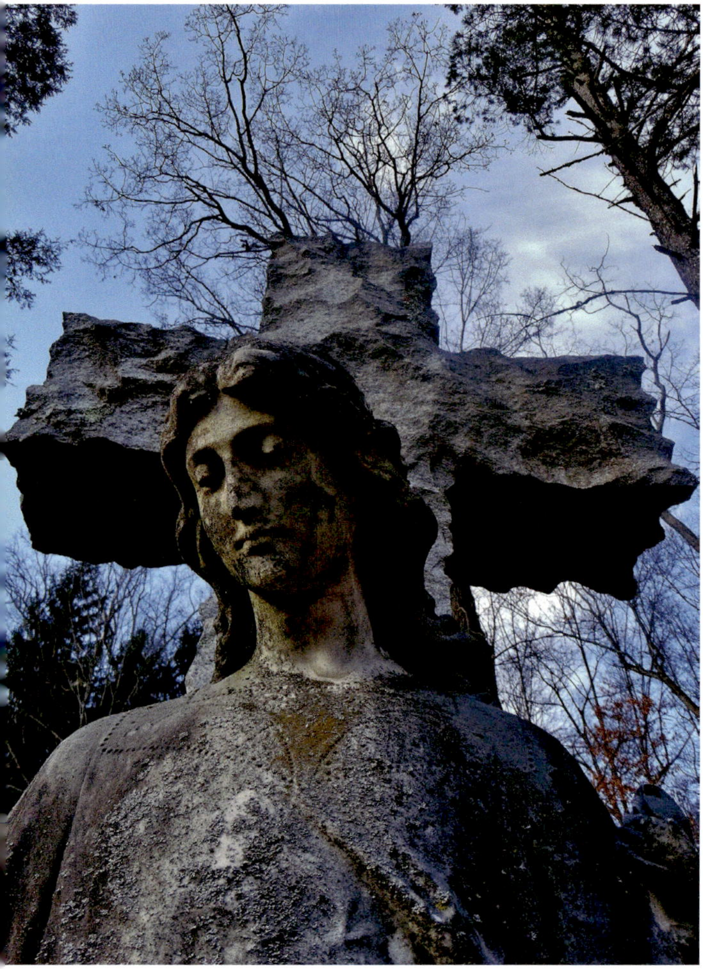

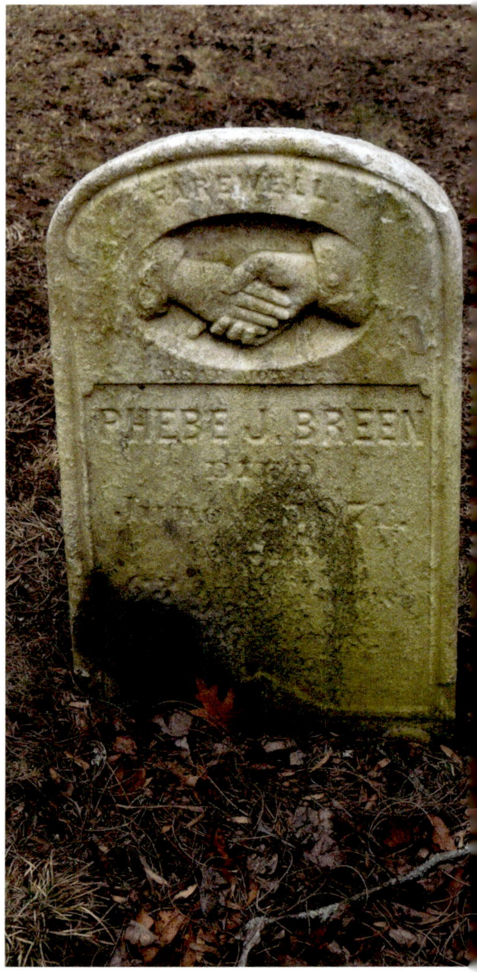

Above left: A close shot of George W. West's memorial reveals a haunting face. West (1847–1908) was a Superintendent of Motive Power for the New York, Ontario & Western Railway.

Above right: Farewell, Phebe J. Breen.

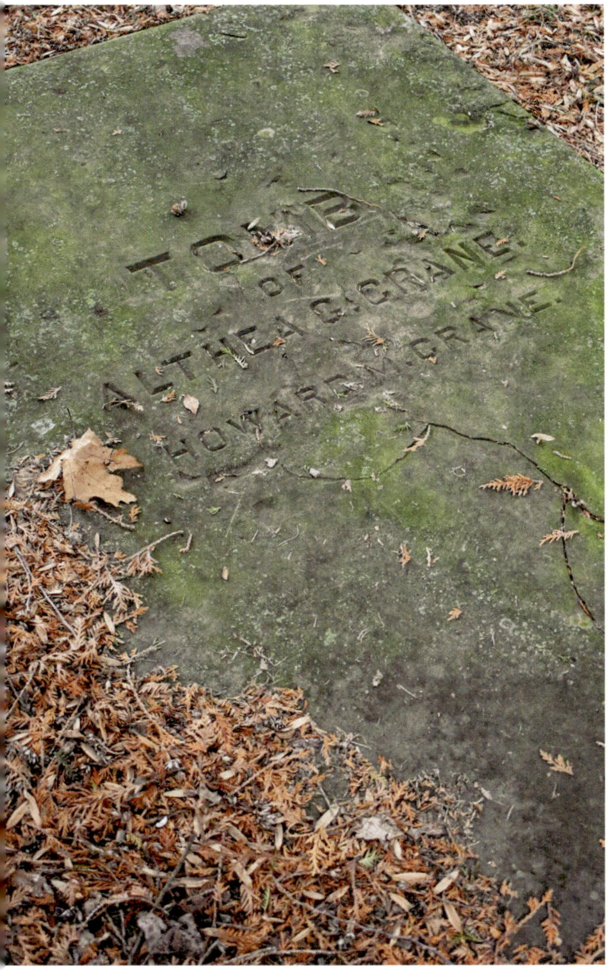

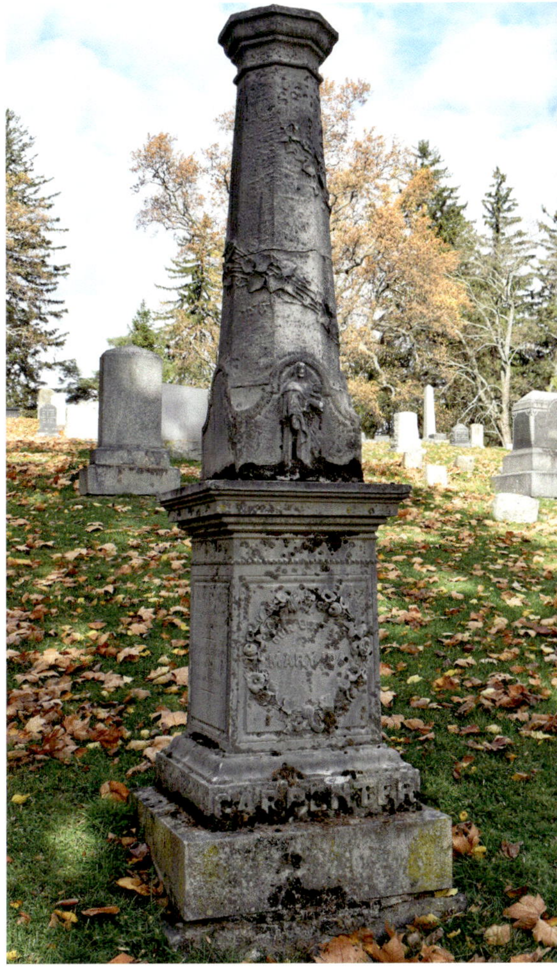

Above left: Buried in the same tomb, Althea Crane (1866–1890) and Howard Crane (1876–1877) were siblings.

Above right: A beautiful and delicate stone was created in memory of Mary Ida.

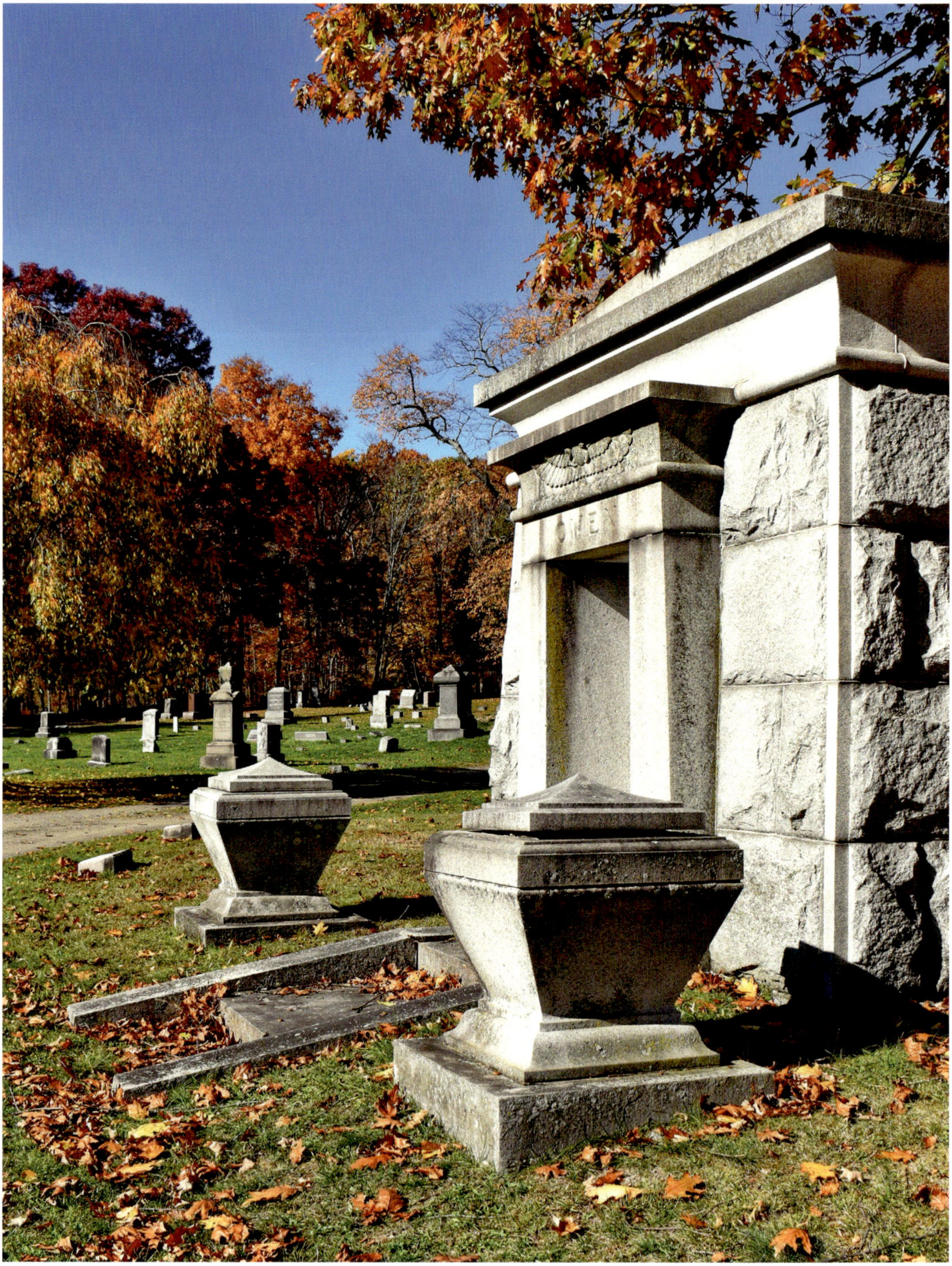

The Owen mausoleum has Egyptian Revival influences in its design. The symbol above the door shows a pair of wings with a circle and twin cobras, which is indicative of Egyptian style.

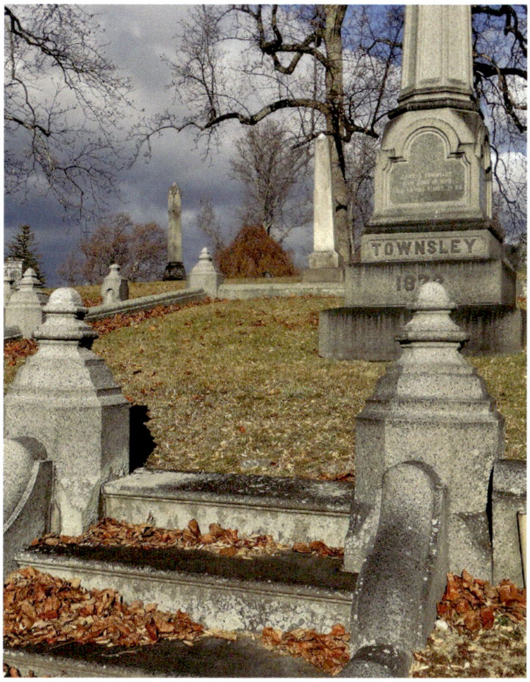

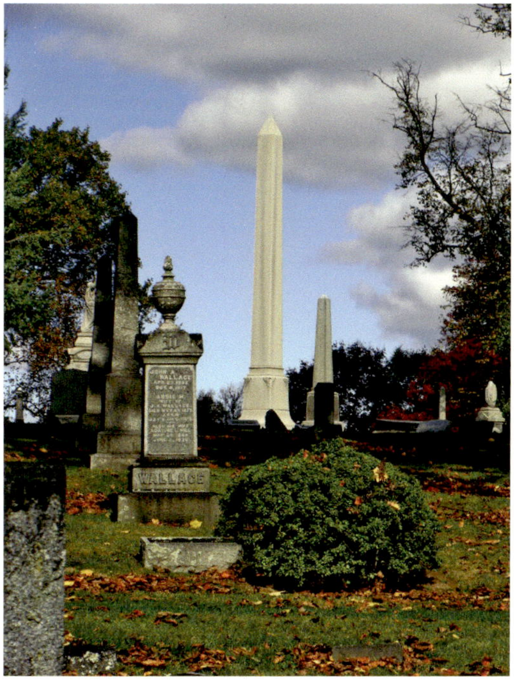

Above left: The view is dotted with obelisks behind the dignified Townsley plot.

Above right: The storms clouds are rolling in on a blustery autumn day.

Right: Hillside is a peaceful home to many living things, too!

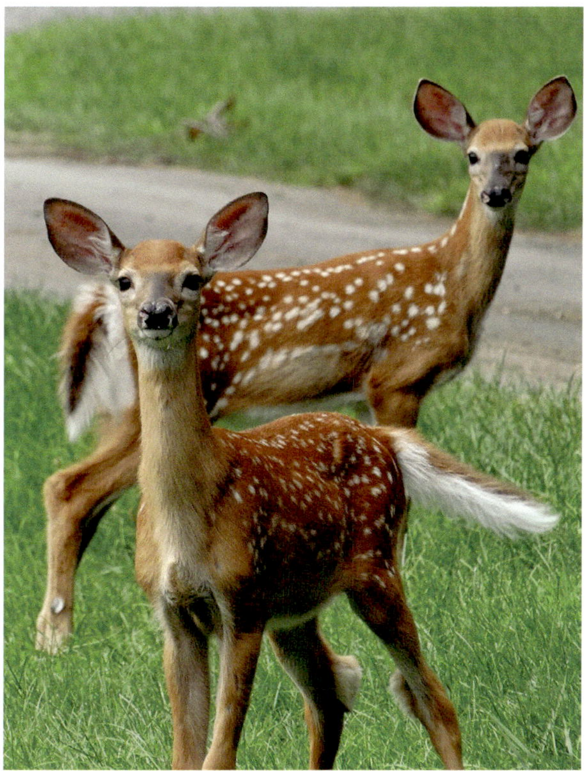

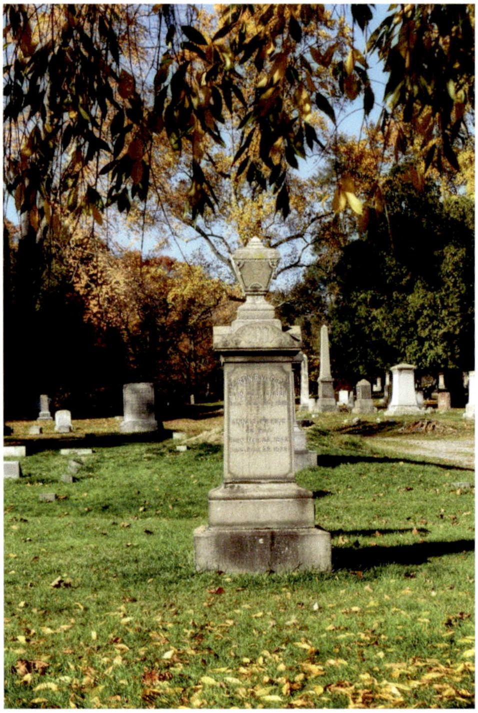

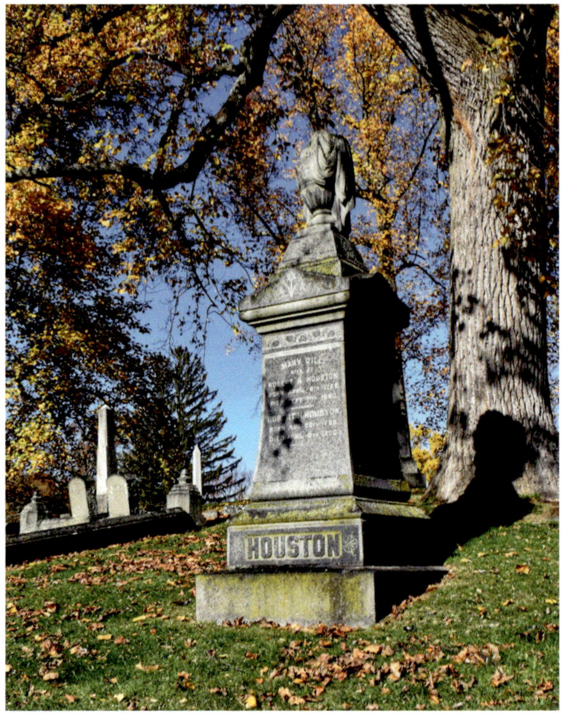

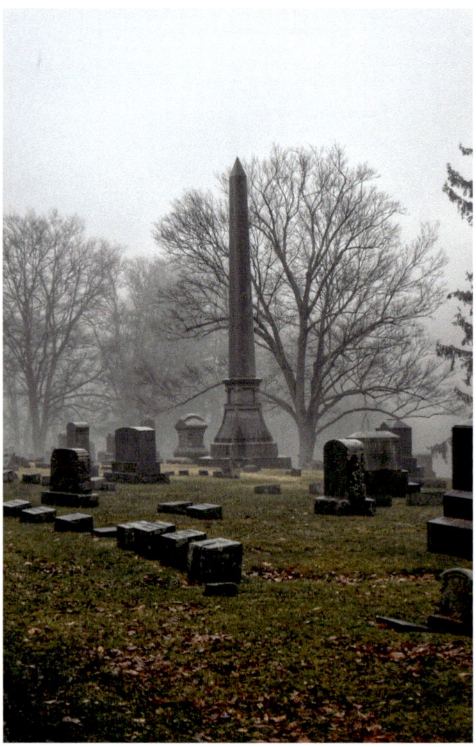

Above left: The Van Fleet grave is framed by a lacey patch of foliage.

Above right: Robert H. Houston (1798–1890) was a tanner and a farmer who contributed greatly to Middletown's prosperity.

Left: The giant obelisk of Timothy Wheat Horton (1819–1897) looms out of the mist. Timothy is the brother of J. M. Horton.

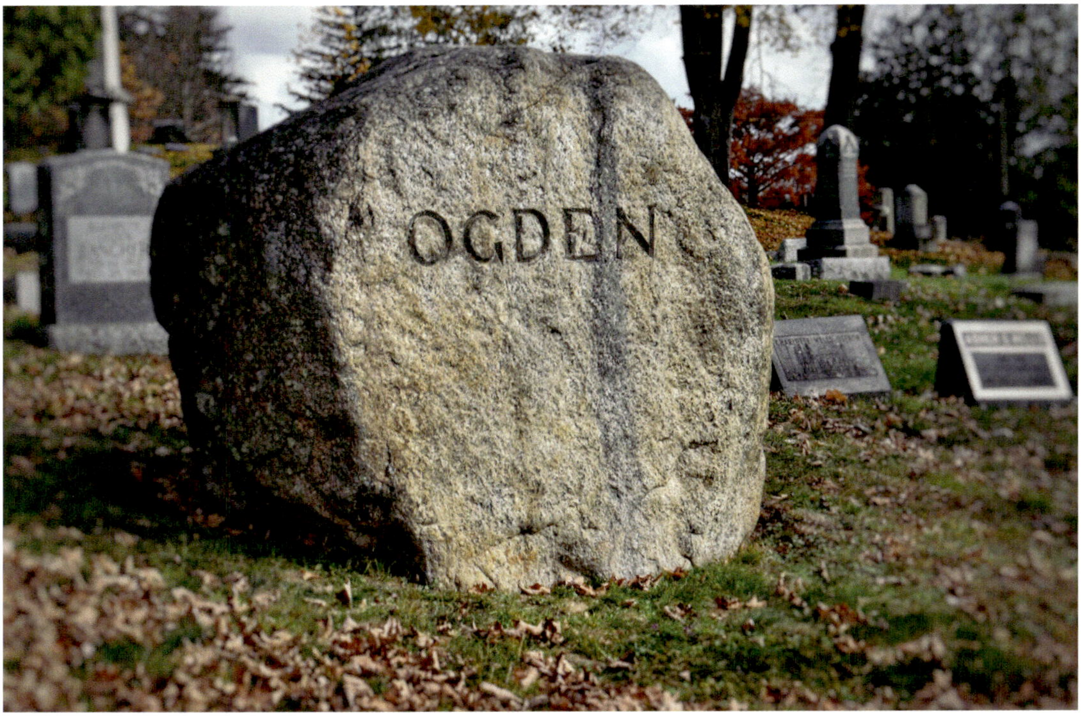

A boulder monument marks the graves of the Ogden family.

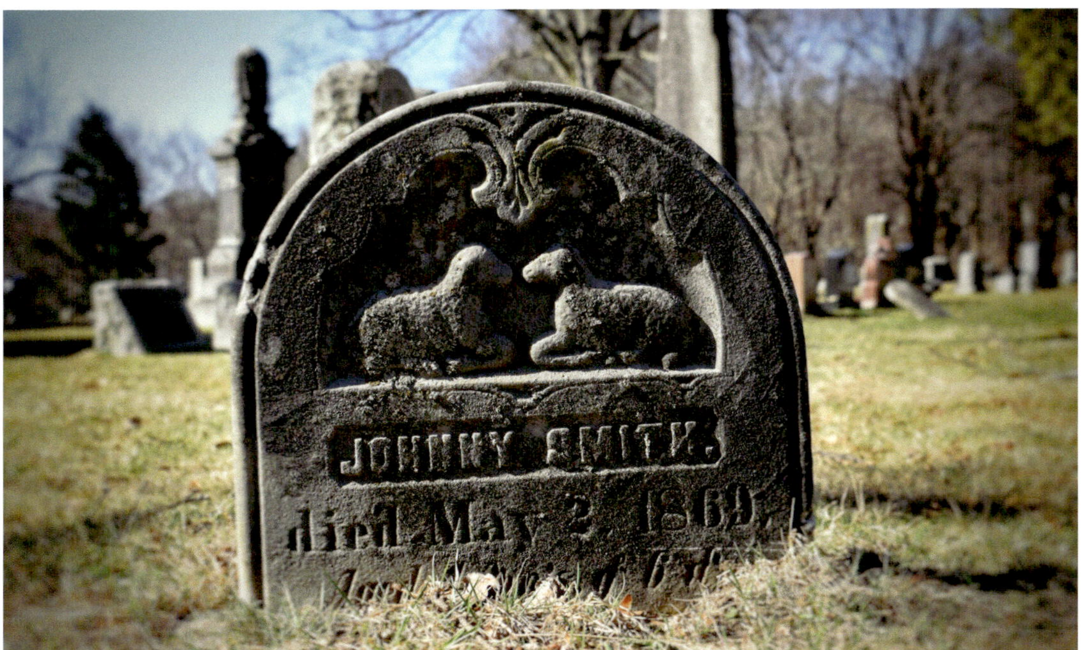

The little stone of Johnny Smith is decorated with lambs.

Author's Note

The first time I wandered into Hillside, I was captivated. Years later and after a myriad of visits, I am still enthralled. The more research I do, the more fascinating the cemetery becomes. I wanted to write this book fifteen years ago; during that time, I received help and support from Mr. Benedict, who has run the cemetery for countless years, and the Historical Society of Middletown. I can't guarantee they remember speaking to me so many years ago, but thank you. I've never forgotten your kindness.

Thank you to my lifelong friend, Sheryl, who endured all kinds of weather and weirdness to join me on my cemetery trips. There were a few graves we weren't able to locate, but that's ok. That just leaves a reason for more adventures in the future.

Thank you to my husband who listened with enthusiasm to my countless stories about tombstones and those buried beneath them.

A big thank you to the dedicated people who have worked and are continuing to work hard to keep Hillside amazing for so many generations to appreciate.

To help keep Hillside's legacy protected, you can also donate:

Hillside Cemetery Corporation
50 Mulberry Street
Middletown, New York 10940
(845) 343-5534

Thank you for reading!